**The Core of Steel Series**
Core of Steel The Beginning: Unconform
Core of Steel Book 1: Going Home
Core of Steel Book 2: Compatibility
Core of Steel Book 3 coming soon

Website
www.truthredux.com

# CORE OF STEEL BOOK 2

# COMPATIBILITY
## Who is for you?

Penni Mannas Diefendorf

# CONTENTS

CHOICES

WRAPPING UP

# PREFACE

The Core of Steel series and the corresponding workshop, Creating Capable Consciousness, are geared towards unraveling the tangled web we have woven around ourselves and bringing us simply to the truth of who we are and the reality of the world around us.

Once we have arrived at this place, we can then settle in and reinforce the attributes that give us the greatest satisfaction, and we can consistently choose the things that bring us our greatest joys. As this way of being becomes second nature to us, we come fully into ourselves. This is our *Core of Steel*. The person we are in our true essence, but which is being smothered and diluted by the conflicting messages around us.

*UNCONFORM: Only the conscious thrive* is the beginning of the journey to your core of steel. It aims to strip away the conditionings you take for granted and in many cases, as truth, but which no longer have a place in your life and are in fact, not true for you.

Book 1 of the series, *Going Home: A Roadmap to Fulfillment and Abundance by Finding Your Truth*, starts changing this submergence of you at its foundation.

It takes you further towards finding the self that you have lost or perhaps never knew. This is the first critical step to living the life of your dreams: to find out who you truly are and what your true dreams are.

This book, Book 2 of the series, asks you to examine *all* your relationships in the light of reality. It highlights many of the myths associated with relationships and also the blocks, which are our own mental barriers caused or perpetuated by these myths, so that you can identify and eliminate them entirely from your life.

By redefining many of the "engines" or "elements" that drive relationships and our reactions to people, *Compatibility* shakes up the illusions and misperceptions that lead us into artificial and confusing interactions.

The final book in the series will create similar new paradigms in the sphere of life situations, the world immediately around us and the wider world, so that we choose with full consciousness the life we create for ourselves and our impact on our world. This is the final piece of the puzzle of our lives, which will puzzle us no longer, but instead becomes an adventure that we actively direct and participate in with joy.

The Core of Steel series represents each stage of our journey to being strong and true versions of ourselves in the ideal sequence.

The answers and clarity you get about yourself, your people and your world, build upon each other with each successive book.

Do not miss a step. And try not to read them out of sequence. It will result in potentially great solutions realised at the wrong time, without the right resources and thus imperfectly applied.

Success at life can be easily and effortlessly arrived at. Just take it step by step. Find yourself — and then trust yourself.

.

# INTRODUCTION

Let me tell you a funny story which contains all sorts of relationship lessons and perhaps some you might least expect!

Once upon a time, a chap came to our gate asking for money or handouts of some description. My Mother, being of the charitable belief that money received from honest work is much better for the soul than unearned providence, suggested that he do a spot of gardening for her in exchange for her contributing to his welfare.

And so it was arranged quite amicably that he transplant my Mother's precious bulbs to a more favourable spot – a task that had been pending for a while – so both parties were well satisfied with this arrangement.

Sometime later, he reported the work complete and Mum went out to inspect it. There in neat and tidy rows were blades of green in the exact formation she expected and so with great willingness, she handed over the promised sum and considered it all a good day's work.

Several days passed during which she would look on the patch of bulbs with pride and joy and imagine all the colourful blossoms that were about to spring forth.

Until, that is, the green leaves seemed to go a little limp. Needing some more water or fertilizer perhaps? Perhaps they were going through transplant shock?

A few more days passed and then the leaves withered and died altogether.

When Mum went to pull them up to see what the matter was, she came up with only leaves in her hand! He had neatly snipped the leaves off the bulbs and pocketed the bulbs themselves to be sold for further gain.

Watching from the sidelines, it was utterly comical to get reports going from what a splendid fellow this was and what a wonderful job he had done and how fulfilling it was to have helped a fellow human being to feel better about themselves, to intense dismay that he could do such a thing.

Not to mention Mum being abjectly aggrieved at the loss of all those bulbs.

It was really very funny and still brings a grin to my face – the idea of him carefully planting the leaves for show and all the while sneaking off with the bulbs.

But this is symptomatic about something that is taken as normal today – that no good deed goes unpunished – which I find abhorrent. And also, that you can basically trust no one, which is a very sad and unsustainable state of affairs.

However, these are not the lessons.

This is: there are very many relationships around us that have no roots, no bulbs, no depth to sustain them.

And they are characterised by them needing a lot of care, attention, water and fertilizer. But with all that, they still wither away because the basic fundamentals required for health and growth are absent.

And yet because they "look" green and healthy on the surface, we continue to spend, in some cases, significant effort to keep them alive when, like those leaves without bulbs, they are doomed to die.

In the light of this, it is absolutely critical to examine our relationships closely and identify the ones that have life and nourishment within them and the ones that take life and energy from us.

### Who is around you?

When we think of relationships our minds immediately leap to friends, partners, family, and colleagues. But in truth, we have a relationship with each and every person we encounter along the way of life.

If we do not believe this, then we discount, to our detriment, the impact ephemeral associations might have on our lives .

The ease or difficulty with which you navigate your life is inextricably bound up in how you relate to people, how you regard them, and therefore, how you treat them.

It also depends on who you allow into your life, what are the parameters by which you gauge the fitness of your associations, and how you maintain the balance and health of your connections.

The list of relationships begins in order of proximity with your immediate family: spouse, partner, and children or your family of origin, basically, who you live with. It expands to include extended family, close friends, colleagues, acquaintances, and ends with all and sundry whom you come across in daily life.

That's a whole lot of people. If you're a very busy person, that just might be all of humanity. We've got our work cut out for us!

As a minimum guiding principle in the sea of different moods, temperaments, cultures, and attitudes, it bears remembering:

Every dog has its day
Every man his finest hour
So be careful what you say
When you think you are in power

That's the absolute minimum, I hope we are all very much beyond that by the end of this book.

### Bubbles of happiness

What is your idea of ideal relationships?

We all want to be loved, taken care of and nourished. But what does that mean for you?

Do you know, have you considered, what it is you require that would give you that feeling?

Do you think it is even possible to have no conflict, stress and unpleasantness in your life?

How are your relationships with *everyone* around you? Think about what you would like to be surrounded by and add as a minimum: joy, nourishment, dependability, peacefulness, positivity and enrichment.

How do your interactions fit? Is there a big gap in some areas?

It is a sad fact that we have been coopted into believing that it is our lot to struggle with others, to have to weave about and tolerate behaviour that makes us uncomfortable and distresses us. That injustice and bad judgements, unfairness, and dislocations of reality are par for the course. We even have a number of clichés for this. "Who says life is fair," "All's fair in love and war," and "Bad things happen to good people.'

I aim to turn all of those on their heads.

Life can be fair to you, if you choose it. All is not fair in love and war, and it is up to you to discern the differences. Only good things need happen to good people, period.

What you need is to develop the antenna, judgement and decision making and, of course, have the strong foundation of security in your own identity and values, a.k.a. your Core of Steel, to make it so.

### Who are you?

When we drill right down to the root, the one and only cause of relationship breakdown is dishonesty from the outset.

This may seem like an oversimplification, but it is nevertheless true. Relationships that are grounded in reality and have a true connection on both sides do not break down, no matter what pressures are brought to bear on them.

They ride the changes life brings about outside of the relationship, within it or within the individuals themselves.

These relationships may change and morph as truly healthy relationships do, but the bond and feelings of honest connections are indestructible. This is an absolute fact and something to not only strive for, but a standard to establish within ourselves, so that we do not settle for less.

Think about this for a moment.

If we are not honest about who we are and what we want and we meet a person who is not honest about who they are and what they want, then the relationship begins and is built on an illusion, which is spun out by erroneous thinking and feeling.

This is exacerbated further when we each look at the other with a disconnect from the truth. We focus on particular elements or facets that appeal to us, see what we want to see, extrapolate that to encompass their whole personality and blissfully block out the rest.

Once rude reality intrudes in the form of actions or behaviour we cannot continue to ignore, this perfect picture starts to disintegrate from either or both sides and there is nothing left to fill the void. The relationship ends with heartbreak and baggage.

This scenario holds true for all relationships: business, personal, and family.

It holds true when people knowingly deceive themselves and others. Because there are limits to even the best fabrications. Time and the effort of weaving tales will begin to break it down at some point.

At this juncture, I want to reiterate that the rightness of our relationships is predicated on our honesty with and knowledge of ourselves.

Having said that, I want to strongly recommend that if you have not read *Going Home,* Book 1 of this series, put this down now and read that first.

We need a very clear and strong understanding of ourselves before we can even begin to try to understand and sort out our relationship with others.

You are about to understand why.

The first inkling we get that our relationships are not as they should be is when we cannot fully be ourselves with people, and "people" here covers the whole range of our social contacts. Maybe you are OK with your immediate family, but a little bit artificial with your social circle. Or vice versa.

If you don't know who you really are, this is going to be hard to establish, but it is critically important. If you are a different person with different people — who is the real you? Do you see the problem?

In one of the discussion groups that truthredux.com hosts from time to time, we discussed this precise topic: "How can we be 'real' in relationships."

The first thing we discussed was *why* this is so important and why sometimes, even knowing that it is vital, we hide who we are or soft pedal what we are thinking.

What blocks us from being genuine, and whatever it is, is it valid?

The collective short answer to the last question was a definite no, whatever the reason, it is never valid.

Because most of us had experienced the downside of professing one thing and then being faced with the necessity of owning up to actually being or feeling another.

In particular, when we discussed why we struggle to be real or show our true self and feelings, what came up was fear that we would not be accepted as we are and fear of our emotions being misconstrued or misrepresented. Sometimes, we subverted our truth out of deference to other people or to avoid an awkward situation.

At the end of the discussion, we came to the inevitable conclusion that no matter what, if we cloaked ourselves, deceptively, with what we believed might be acceptable or loved or rewarded, we could not have genuine relationships.

We therefore could not ever be secure in them, because who, exactly, are the people in our lives having a relationship with? It's not us — "we" are buried under layers of fabrication.

And if we don't have genuine relationships, they will, one by one, fail. They do not have the flimsiest foundation on which to survive.

So before you even begin to examine your relationships, know yourself.

# LOST IN THE MYTHS

# 1

## MYTHING THE POINT

**L**et us start by blasting through some relationship myths. And if you have any not detailed here, then do a reality check of your own to see if you can get to the truth.

Most of these myths are deeply ingrained in our collective consciousness, such that we accept them as unquestioned reality. We see no great flaw in jealousies, possessiveness, game playing, relationship "strategies," quid pro quo, and an unending litany of drama and crises.

All of which are inspired by one or the other of these myths. The truth lies in recognizing the essence of ourselves and others and that these essential selves are independent of each other and not necessarily compatible. But they are as they are. If we see and address the reality of the people around us and not through the framework of any of the following, we will then be equipped to handle any other myth that comes our way — either our own or others.

### The people around you are "yours"
This has got to be the most infamous myth of all and the most rampant. Even the least possessive person probably has a streak or a

wishfulness of this as a reality.

Society has been set up to perpetuate this myth. We have marriage, exclusive relationships, nuclear families, businesses — all of which are set up to give us the comfortable notion of "units." Once we are in a "unit," whichever it is, we are secure; they are "ours," we are "theirs," and we are set for life.

I read this somewhere a long time ago, that the greatest hurts come from people we know who are most similar to us. And here is where the belief of similarity starts — that "our" people know us, are in our corner, and it is our right that they do well by us and be there for us.

All of this is, indeed, possible and of course, highly desirable, but not in the manner of this myth.

It behooves us to ring the changes between "owning" and "belonging."

Owning is the tone of this myth. It is the prime reason for ill-treatment in relationships where:

- bosses can be rude and inconsiderate of staff
- romantic partners can be insulting and hurtful
- family can be manipulative and unsupportive
- friends can be absentee and frenemies

It is in the belief that work, loyalty, and remaining in the relationship are "owed" because of the nature of the relationship, because of ownership.

If we accept their ownership, these unbalanced situations continue without us questioning the rationale of it.

The healthy reality is "belonging." This is the happy situation in which no persuasion or guile is required to maintain the relationship.

People come together and stay together because their needs are perfectly met, and they as individuals and the group or "unit" thrives and grows. The freedom to be is unhampered by ownership, the artificial net cast to actively contain a group or entity, but is instead fostered by a sense of belonging and a wish to be right in that spot.

One of the reasons we hang on to relationships that have moved well past their sell-by dates is because we think it's "ours." That we are entitled to whatever it is we feel it should be giving us, even though it is not at all fulfilling our requirements — it's just that we think it *should*.

### There are "rules" for every stage or phase

Following closely on the heels of thinking of our associates as possessions, we have phases in our scheme of things from introduction to acquisition. This is another product of social and business conditioning, that has been twisted out of all understanding.

There are natural ebbs and flows in all human relating, the keyword there being *natural*. When it becomes unnatural and strained is when life, situations, and people are expected to conform to an enforced rule.

Otherwise known as "the games people play." So there is the research phase, the introductory phase, the getting-to-know-you phase, the now-you-work-for-me, are-intimate-with-me, are-family phase, the this-is-not-working phase, etc.

And everyone, has their own version of what rules hold good for each phase. There are a host of articles on how to behave, what to say, how to salvage something to go with each phase, and some of it very good and sensible advice, no doubt, but all of it perpetuating the idea of "rules" and best practices in relating.

The real truth is there are no rules, ever. Save the ones you and the people around you agree work for yourselves and the situation at any given time. And those rules, for want of a better word, or shall we say understandings, should never require a change of personality and way of being for the sole purpose of making the "rules" work. Does that make sense?

The tail must never wag the dog.

Certainly, there is never the necessity for a dislocation of relating or an artificiality of relating as people evolve, such as when a colleague is promoted, or a family member gets married / divorced, or friends become lovers, or vice versa.

And yet, it happens time and again because of this myth. Because somehow overnight, we are dealing with a whole different person as a result of their changed status. Incidentally, we do this to ourselves as well.

This is all kinds of wrong and very often leads to traumatic reversals of fortune and relationships needlessly.

We don't live in "stages." We are not "phases." We are people living one continuous life experience, and it is vastly confusing to be shifting gears as is required by this myth. Don't believe in it.

### People "owe" you something

This is a very insidious myth because we know logically and intellectually that we are not owed anything. If only through it being dinned or drilled into our heads by the people around us and our life experiences, we can be very sure that this is true.

And yet, every time we are bitterly disappointed that something didn't come through or that someone let us down, we can be equally sure that this myth was alive and well within us.

Sometimes, it might well be justified along the lines of, we've worked long and hard for it, we deserve it. Or we've given whatever we've had, we've created the right circumstances, personality, pathway, so we are entitled to success, a great relationship and abundance. And all things being equal, we will be right.

The tricky part is in the entitlement mindset. We might be proved right, we may be proved wrong. Whichever the case, if we buy into this myth and believe something will naturally follow, we are setting ourselves up for a big fall.

The difference in attitude is the difference between "demanding" and "commanding." If we have an "I'm owed this" mindset then we are demanding and will be perceived as such.

Not surprisingly, such an attitude tends to meet with some pushback. Especially so if it is not backed up by substance.

Alternatively, if there is substance and truth and they are coupled with a "commanding" attitude though not in the militaristic sense, there is every possibility of achieving what you deserve — in a good way. This kind of attitude adopts the position that if what you are offering is worthy, it will be taken up. This applies to skill sets for a job or a relationship.

It also applies to the regard you garner from others. Trust, respect, love. You cannot demand these, but you can command them by being worthy of them. Big difference.

### Giving more will solve all problems

So despite the previous two myths, you are now in a relationship or job or family, and things aren't going as happily as you would like. Perhaps you are actively uneasy or maybe even downright miserable.

All the evils of not seeing clearly in the first place, or even in the second place, are now at your doorstep.

The boss is incompetent, your colleagues are politicking, your partner is revolting, your family doesn't care, your kids have run amok.

All in all, your relationships are in shambles, and it's not going to make you look good on your resume or among your social circle. It is also making daily life decidedly uncomfortable.

Ah! There is always this myth. Pour in more time at work, compensate for the boss. Try to understand your partner, and change yourself. Do more for your family. Take the flak for your kids.

In short, exert yourself to the maximum, and the situation will eventually turn around.

This myth is the granddaddy of all second chances and thirds, ad infinitum. The grand adventure of turning a sow's ear into a silk purse.

And, as with all good myths, there is some iota of truth hiding in there. One person in the mists of time was probably able to turn this to good account. But reality is lost in half-truths and foggy logic. A spade will remain a spade no matter how much you wish it to be a bulldozer. And that's the bottom line.

By all means, be as generous and big-hearted as you can be. This is what makes the world go 'round. Just don't do it with the idea that it will change someone else. You know who is the only person who can do that.

## Your relationship(s) will make everything better

The belief in this myth, which is the second degree of the previous myth, could be the reason some of us immerse ourselves in mindless social activity. Or work all hours God sends and then some. Or are serial and relentless monogamists. Or endlessly hanker after a child or a pet.

We believe that any or all of these will improve our lives in just the way we want. We look to these relationships and connections to brighten the routine and lack lustre of our lives, help us achieve our goals, fulfill us romantically and financially.

The highest degree of this myth is that any relationship or combination thereof will complete us. This might be compounded by a belief in soul mates, one purpose in life, and fairy tales.

Don't get me wrong, I love fairy tales and happy endings. I even believe in synchronicity and serendipity. I just don't recommend allowing any of these to trump reality. The converse is true – when you ground yourself in reality, serendipity and synchronicity are very reliable and amazingly frequent.

But back to this myth, the reality is, if you are incomplete within yourself, there is precious little, read nothing, that will complete you in this world.

### You must fill your "role"

We are obsessed by labels and roles. We step into a new life, and we think we should suddenly become another person.

If we are promoted at work, we should become more serious, distant with our former peers, take up schmoozing with the higher-ups, and adopt an attitude becoming of our elevated status.

If we enter into a committed relationship, we should give up our friends, give up our previous activities, meld into some sort of single entity with our partner that excludes the rest of the world and generally leave behind our "old" life.

If we have children, we don the cap of parenthood. and no matter what professional standing we had achieved earlier, that is washed away and subsumed under the almighty weight of our new identity.

If we join a new social circle, we bend over backwards to conform to the frequency and types of get-togethers that are the norm, we listen to conversations we are inwardly cringing at and we put up with attitudes far removed from what we could approve of.

If we don't believe this ourselves, sometimes the people around us try to impose the role.

I remember once being told, by another woman, no less, that I wasn't a good partner as I didn't iron shirts and cook. After shaking the feeling that I was in a bad reproduction of Cinderella, I was able to heave my jaw off the floor and have a good laugh.

Really! There's no accounting for people.

It's this fit-into-a-role myth. That if we just show up and be ourselves, something dire is going to happen. That if our life changes and our lifestyle changes, we should too. There's that tail wagging the dog again.

This, of course, points to a deeper problem. If life's changes are causing a schism in ourselves — that might mean our lives are beyond our control. That we are not initiating changes and bringing about the life that we want, it's more like life is happening to us and we are along for the ride.

Combine that with the perceived need to contort ourselves out of shape to fit a "role," and that's a recipe for disaster.

## Your relationship will never change

By some happy chain of events, you are now in a highly satisfying and well-paying job, blissful relationship, and harmonious family. Well, hallelujah! And well done.

Be wary though of this myth. That nothing will change. This is not confined to negative changes; positive changes require adjustments to be made as well.

If you buy into this myth, a dogmatic and entrenched attitude sets in. This works, we are all happy, if it ain't broke don't fix it. By the way, that last theory should only apply to appliances and fixtures!

If you hold onto the status quo at all costs, even to the extent of believing that it shouldn't change, then you are very likely to miss the small tell-tale signs along the way, that your reality is shifting and the people around you are changing.

Back to an idea expressed in Book 1, crises don't happen overnight. Massive change doesn't happen overnight. It is effected in the small things, which if not taken into account earlier, become the overwhelming avalanche of loss.

Pay attention, especially if you are very happy with a relationship in your life, that you don't fall prey to this myth.

People change, therefore, relationships must change. It follows.

The truly worthwhile relationships shift, change, deepen and get better all the time – regardless of space, distance and time.

**Relationships will last forever**

It is sad, but true. Nothing lasts forever.

There must be some interruption, through some cause, sooner or later.

The downside of this myth, when in a bad relationship, is that it saps hope and courage.

If you're in a bad job, it extinguishes the light at the end of the tunnel.

The biggest problem with this, though, is that it causes complacency or lethargy.

We feel at liberty to get sloppy, inconsiderate, take things for granted or be overcome by inertia. All of which are virtually guaranteed to explode this myth by bringing about the very ending we did not believe in.

Life is precious. Our relationships are precious. And they are both as fragile or as strong as we create them to be. But neither lasts forever, and we must not at any time give rein to this myth, not in a morbid sort of way, but in an enriching, live-every-moment-and-experience kind of way.

This is a great approach to most things in life.

**Relationships are hard work**

This is a myth that has manifested itself strongly over the last few decades. That we must "work" at relationships. No longer are they recreational or sources of joy and nourishment. Nope. They are work.

It is ridiculous. But firmly wedged into our overall psyche. We are convinced that struggle and strife are par for the course.

As a result, we are imprisoned by this delusion and just accept that we are stuck with:

- Dealing with unreasonable bosses
- Covering for less-competent colleagues
- Changing ourselves for incompatible partners
- Taking on the sins of our parents, siblings, children
- Befriending people we don't value
- Befriending people who don't value us
- Settling for unrewarding relationships in general

This, we say with forlorn conviction, is life. The French, of course, say it much more prettily — *c'est la vie.* Same awful consequences.

We have bought and sold this myth such that effortless partnerships, businesses that care, and considerate employers are things of legend and modern-day miracles. What a sorry pass!

Turn this on its head. If a relationship is difficult, entertain the idea that it is not supposed to be, as in exist in your sphere of things to do.

This does not preclude actively trying to improve your relationships. It does require, at a minimum, to abandon this idea that something as potentially joyful as your communications with the people around you should be "work."

### People have the power to hurt you

In actuality, nobody has the power to do anything to you save what you grant them. And save by brute force, of course. So be mindful of the situations you put yourself in.

And for the latter, take a course in self-defense. Seriously.

We want to approach every relationship and potential relationship with our eyes wide open until we are sure of our ground. Even when we are sure and we trust our circle implicitly, we cannot put all our dependence on others. We must at all times be aware of the spaces between us.

And sometimes those spaces mean that our interests don't coincide. If we have this awareness, we can step lightly away from hurt and disappointment.

We are able to realise at a fundamental level that each of us is on our own journey and allow it to be so.

Chief among the resources to blast this myth, is the inner strength that will allow us to stand alone when we need to.

This is irreplaceable especially when we are called upon to stand up for our convictions, to not support someone on point of principle, or to stand firm in the face of manipulation or emotional blackmail.

If you understand very clearly that every time you are hurt, you have given up your own power and given someone else the power to hurt you, you will very soon start reasserting your own autonomy over your feelings and a very different picture will emerge.

### You are not responsible
Following on from that and the best one of all that makes all the rest possible. We are not

responsible.

We can carp on and on about how we can never get steady work, everlasting romance, obedient children, and the like. At any given time and at various points in our life this may each be true and, even with the best will and attitude in the world, beyond our control.

However. If all of the above are repeated refrains in your life. If you feel undervalued, unloved, disrespected, and disregarded, ask yourself if you hold yourself well and truly responsible.

To paraphrase Lady Bracknell: to be at outs with a few people may be regarded as a misfortune, to be at outs with all of them looks like carelessness to me.

That's Lady Bracknell from Oscar Wilde's *The Importance of Being Earnest,* an excellent take on the vagaries of human behaviour.

# 2

# TACKLING OUR BLOCKS

The reason we prefer to apply myths to our lives is because they neatly encompass and explain what we believe to be overwhelming difficulties and insurmountable problems. It is far easier to accept that this is the way things are and that everyone goes through rough patches, than to examine what exactly is going on in our own rough patches and acknowledge it.

Better not to look too closely in case, heaven forbid, we have to do something about it.

The "something" must always include changing an elusive aspect about ourselves or our situation that we feel ill-equipped to do. Or that is bound to make us dreadfully ill at ease in the process. And so, we don't mind at all if we skip this step.

The idea that we can't handle change or that we will find ourselves wanting is, in actuality, not true. Because, as has been found time and time again, when we hit rock bottom, all sorts of hidden talents and resourcefulness come to the fore to get us out.

So why on earth do we put up with unsatisfactory relationships when we have the capacity within us to do so much better for ourselves?

We limit ourselves and our capacity for happiness through a string of blocks and fears that are no more real than monsters under the bed.

If we recognize any of these blocks that are to some degree hiccupping our efforts to move forward, we must crash through them to be able to adopt the ideas and take the steps that follow later on in this book.

### Preserving the status quo

It is said that given time and necessity, one can become used to having hot coals between the toes. While I have no intention of putting this theory to the test myself, we see evidence of it all around us, where acutely uncomfortable situations seem to thrive with the support of the very people that they are most uncomfortable for!

This is passing strange to me.

And I lay the fault at the door of this need to preserve the status quo.

Far be it for us to raise a flag or blow the whistle on something that is completely out of line because, for sure, doing so is going to rock a great many boats. Even if said boats are as leaky as sieves.

The most obvious deployment of this block, though, is when things are ho-hum. Nothing terribly wrong, but definitely nothing right. We can get along with being mildly uncomfortable or dissatisfied. This is the reason that most positive change comes out of an extreme chain of unfortunate life events or a single huge trauma.

Well, if that's what you're waiting for, I put it to you that you will regret this impetus for change wildly when it happens.

But a lot of the time, that is exactly what all of us do. We wait for the last minute, we put off actions until they become critical, we push ourselves to the do-or-die point. What we are doing all along is holding on to "things as they are" until we are forced to change or take action.

What we don't realise is, in doing so, we relinquish the control we have on any action we have to take. And the energy that could have been spent in formulating plans to better our associations is instead wasted in trying to preserve relationships that should not be preserved.

The result of being compelled to take action, or being forced into another situation is that we are very often launched from the frying pan into the fire without our explicit approval.

We have not granted ourselves the time or space to consider what we want as change and therefore have to accept what is imposed on us. More hot coals that we then accustom ourselves to in honour of this idea of status quo.

### Fear of the unknown

We have lots of motivation to hang on to the status quo if we have this block. Better the devil we know than the angel we don't, we say with perfectly straight faces.

Devils or angels — I'll take unknown angels

any day of the week. Hopefully, if you have done all the exercises in *Going Home*, you will too. You will have greatly reduced your fears all around or at least have found a way to get them under control.

It is reasonable to be wary of what you don't know, and it is a step in the right direction if you are aware that this is blocking you.

We had an interesting conversation at a round table meeting I attended recently. It was on exactly this point.

There were two seemingly opposite views. One person held that if he feared something, he took it as a warning from himself that that choice was too dangerous and that therefore, he should not get involved.

The other point of view was that fear of what lay ahead, in other words, the unknown was merely an indication that he didn't have sufficient knowledge or information to proceed and so he should set about getting it and then proceed as planned.

I would venture that both are correct. Sometimes, the risk to our hearts and well-being are too great, and if after some investigation and thought we find it is indeed not a good investment of ourselves, we should desist.

At other times, we may find that in the balance a friendship, business partnership, or relationship may have more joys than woes and we proceed. In both cases, though, we are required to face the unknown and make an assessment.

To remain where we are because we cannot do that is to remain stagnant and a tool of life and others.

### Fear of change
A little different from not knowing, is when we know full well what awaits us or what the possibilities are, we just fear taking the leap and actually taking action.

You have this fear if you endlessly plan for future action but don't actually execute any. You know what you have to do, you know it is essential to do it, but you just don't do it.

And of course it is frustrating. You can see your bright new shiny life ahead of you, but just that touch out of reach.

So why hold back?

Perhaps it is the ramifications of all that future life entails; you don't really want to preserve the status quo, but you worry endlessly about all the things you'll have to do differently or all the ways you'll have to be different.

So you chew over all the possible consequences and potentialities of taking that first step in the effort to buy time to not take it. That, of course, perpetuates itself, 'til you literally talk yourself out of it.

This is the big danger of this block. It is so reasonable. And at the same time, we can tell ourselves that we are doing something. We are planning, we are thinking. But we are actually not *changing* anything.

## Labeling

This is a great one, and the cornerstone of a great deal of bullying and abuse. The "Label."

This is applied with equal liberality from both sides of relationships.

On one side: I am so-and-so, therefore I must be obeyed, catered to, indulged no matter how unreasonable or destructive.

And on the other: You are so-and-so, therefore I must submit, take abuse, nurture you, no matter how unpleasant or soul-destroying it is for me.

Wow!

And society actively encourages these divisions of labour. Parents are frowned on for disciplining their kids, families are judged for internal discord, partners and businesses are stigmatized for breakdowns, and at the same time bullies get away with, sometimes literally, murder.

Any infringement of the labels we unanimously accept is seen as "wrong" and therefore, we avoid infringing them at all costs.

Of course this is very far from ideal, but what is even more wrong is the belief that all these labels hold good in every situation.

There's a great deal of grief that could be avoided if people had the freedom to say, "Guess what? I'm not a label and these conditions are not mine and don't fit, so I'm going to cast them off."

The good news is everyone does — have that freedom, I mean.

What is required to exercise it is a Core of Steel that will gift you with a blissful disregard for what other uninvolved parties have to say.

## Worthiness

The saddest pass a human being can come to is to believe that they are not worthy of better.

With all the hype and discussion about self-esteem and confidence, this is very often pushed underground and not thought about, because, of course, we are worthy.

And yet, there is a small voice in us that says, I don't deserve it, I can't handle it.

And so we baulk at putting ourselves first. Making time to consider alternatives to the relationships we have.

If people let us down, we find excuses for why this might be so. We are relieved when people like us or call us up regardless of whether they are truly good for us. Or we are not picky about who we associate with, we are just glad to have "friends" and a social circle.

If we don't believe we are worthy of excellent treatment and respect, we will put up with things like people standing us up, moving goalposts, waffling about critical decisions, gossiping about us, frenemies, reneging on agreements without reason or notice and in general, providing us with stress and insecurity.

A far cry from love and nourishment.

If we can bolster our sense of what we are worth, if we value our own time, mental space and love, then we will give this kind of behaviour the attention it merits: none. And move on to relationships that better reflect who we are and who we are aiming to be.

### Fear of being alone

We are naturally social creatures, some less than others, but we all require some contact with our fellow beings in order to exercise and grow the various facets of our being.

However, at the essence of it, we are alone. There is no *one* person who can "complete" us as we saw in the previous chapter. This is a simple unassailable fact.

If we are shaky within ourselves we look to others to shore us up. When we are not comfortable in our own skin, we look for affirmations and support from our relationships. We *need* relationships. And when we seek and maintain relationships on that basis, we sow the seeds of our own despair.

We will enter into friendships, relationships, and work based on a faulty set of parameters. We will take on projects and people out of a need to just be surrounded by warm bodies. We pretend to give, when all we must do for our own survival is take.

In exchange, we might put up with the most egregious circumstances because we feel it's "fair exchange no robbery." As an example, we might put up with intense loneliness, just to not be alone.

A life based on these parameters must be half lived at best. Unless by some rare good fortune, it evolves through a series of good encounters to a more healthy and independent state.

### Unspoken rules

In addition to rules that are laid on the table, there are a whole host of unspoken rules out there that are made insidious by their lack of expression.

So, how do we know we have infringed an unspoken rule?

There are those uncomfortable silences, the exchange of looks around the room, the scowl from the person in authority. Or it could be the overtly kindly word in your ear, an earnest chat that circumnavigates the point, or ostracisation.

This proves too much to bear to a great many people. So especially when a situation is new, there is an immense drive to tip-toe around, get the lay of the land and not step on any toes. Ever voiced or thought in these terms?

Yup. This is what you're avoiding, the underlying things that cannot be voiced but must be obeyed.

I have often thought that if things cannot be spoken, they must be too unreasonable to be followed. You may feel free to adopt this sentiment and consider what people don't say, but expect you to know in this light.

Very often, abuse and addiction fly under the radar with the help of this nifty little tool. So and so is an addict or child-molester, but he is in such and such position of power, so we can't say anything or call them on it.

There are walls of silence enclosing vast infringements of human rights and miscarriages of justice. These are kept in force through rigorously punishing anyone not marching in tune. As a result, serious dysfunctions go unnoticed and uncorrected.

This is a block that should be overcome or escaped from at all costs.

### Religious beliefs

The world today is rife with actions being taken and lives being lived and lost on the basis of religion.

If we accept or reject relationships based on what our religion says rather than what we feel is right, good, and nourishing, we negate every principle and precept of what that religion actually holds to be true.

For every teaching or rule in religion, there are very good odds you could find something somewhere else in that same religion that counters it. Try it sometime.

This is not contradictory in the least. What it means, quite realistically, is that at any given time, a different rule or perspective should prevail depending on the circumstances, the personalities, and the fairness of the situation.

Most of life's problems arise from implementing the right idea at the wrong time or vice versa. Preserve me from sound principles incorrectly applied.

I do not believe any religion would advocate physical, emotional, or psychological violence, or cruelty or suffering. No matter how many quotes can be quoted. This is probably the origin of the saying, the devil quotes scripture for his purpose.

As with all the blocks in this chapter, it is no more or no less irrelevant in mapping out the relationships you wish to have. Nor is it grounds to discount or encourage relationships.

I remember when I was growing up being told that one religion and one religion only held the key to salvation. The idea being that somehow we were better, safer, and more worthy of exaltation.

It happened to be mine, good for me!

This did not bring the comfort I assumed it was intended to. I was utterly horrified at the thought that the rest of my friends who were not signed up, but all excellent human beings in their own right, were going straight down to that warmer place.

Happily, I was able to dismiss this notion out of hand and proceed to make multidenominational friendships without further ado or fear for their immortal souls.

And so it must be. The main purpose of religion is to find peace and joy. A bit hard to do if you're swamped in a morass of lousy relationships.

### Tradition and culture

Yet another power grab to wrest the reins of rational, healthy behaviour from the hands of many and deposit it in the hands of the few.

Tradition and culture have their place in many facets of our lives. There's a soothing richness to etiquette and manners. A quaintness to superstitions and remedies. One place it should not be applied to is as a hindrance in relationships.

There it merely serves as an excuse for bad behaviour. As I write this, we are seeing dreadful outrages perpetrated on people on the basis of "culture." Or perpetrated on them because they bucked said culture and tradition.

It is no wonder that in many cases, this is an insurmountable block. But we cannot have healthy dialogue and nourishing relationships with ourselves and each other if we cannot overcome this.

**3**

# TRAPS FOR THE UNWARY

**B**eyond myths and blocks are some subtle traps: ways of being that derive from them, and other messages from society and our peers. These attributes are equally, if not more powerful than external pressures, for the simple reason that we have taken them on as our own and have given them carte blanche to be.

As a result, they are slightly more difficult to deal with because they require that we 'fess up to our own fallibility and change our way of dealing with people from a very deep-rooted and fundamental place.

It may require us to grow a backbone, take a stand, re-examine what we've been taught, and redefine our behaviour. But, if we can do all of these things honestly, we will create the relationships we dream of.

Surely an excellent exchange.

### Self-effacing
Very often mistakenly substituted for humility, being self-effacing results in being effaced by everyone else as well.

True humility can only come from real strength.

It stems from being so sure and strong in yourself that you do not need the praise and admiration from others, nor any imposed position of power to prove yourself. It does not seek accolades or recognition and if such arrive they do not affect us one way or the other. Likewise with condemnation. Neither results in elevation or degradation, it is a very stable place to be, being humble.

Self-effacing on the other hand is the front of being humble, but hides a deep hopelessness or poor image of yourself. Whatever cloak you cast over it, people around you sense what stems from weakness and what stems from strength.

If you are forever being taken advantage of, asked to do more than your fair share, have a reputation for never being able to say no, take heed of this trap.

All your relationships must start and end with a strong *you* to have any chance at health, growth, and longevity.

Here is a great time to interject one of my favourite jokes.

Chap dials the wrong number without realizing it and says: "Neil?"

And the voice at the other end answers without missing a beat: "No. We bow and scrape, but we do not kneel."

That should be us, bow and scrape, but do not kneel. Come to think of it, I guess we can dispense with bowing and scraping as well in the normal course of things.

## Living vicariously

Or living from the sidelines.

Through some mysterious agent in life, we sometimes find ourselves subverting our own course of life to the people around us. We live through our primary relationships, in other words, our partners, our children, our best friends, or even through our work.

So our joys are someone else's, our friends are someone else's or jointly shared. We live our life and our relationships fused at the hip with someone or the other.

The problem with living through other people is that at some point their thoughts, ideas, and actions are going to depart significantly from our own. What then?

Wrenching change and rude awakenings. Your joy and being was all bound up in someone else and you didn't realise it till they left or changed.

When people say that one person or child or friend is "everything" to them, they had best examine that to see how literally they mean it. An external "everything" might well be a ticking time bomb.

## Turning the other cheek

This is an unholy mix of religious belief and self-effacement that has given rise to a large-scale acceptance and continuance of bad behaviour.

If you believe you should turn the other cheek and allow harm to be done to you, not necessarily physically, but harm of some description, you are deliberately setting yourself up to be misused repeatedly.

Kind of like wearing a sign across your rear-end saying "kick me." And who in their right mind would do that!

So why not respond to the nuances of life with honest and appropriate reactions?

Why instead, when we are at the receiving end of behaviour that has all the impact of a stunning blow to the head, do we smile and nod and refrain from giving the responsible party a severe set down or at the very least make it manifestly clear that we don't appreciate such moves?

It's a dyed-in-the-wool attitude that people have some kind of divine right to be mean and objectionable towards you.

Set your mind at rest. They don't.

### Making allowances

Following on from the thought that everyone must have every opportunity to be as they are, even if that means being utterly intolerable, is the habit of making allowances.

"Johnny is so spirited," we say fondly as the little monster takes a wrecking ball to the house.

Okay, it may not be as extreme as that, but making allowances for behaviour that is unacceptable in any company might as well be.

Someday, when there is time and opportunity, it might be worthwhile to do research on how many parents of murderers said that their children had anger-management problems or a just a nasty temper.

When you make excuses for the people in your

lives, you are doing much more than allowing hurtful behaviour towards you to continue, you are giving them the green light to visit that behaviour on other people and continue it for the rest of their lives.

Of course, the reason we make allowances could be any one of those myths and blocks, but in the final analysis, it is not healthy for the giver and the receiver.

It is like allowing words to be misspelt when children are learning to spell. Doing so sorely missed the point and resulted in a generation of poor spellers. It is now left to their peers in various forums to bemoan this.

### Wooly boundaries

A very, very compelling reason to develop your Core of Steel sooner rather than later.

It is critical to know where your limits are and understand very clearly when you are reaching the farther ends of it in any given situation.

If you have ever suddenly snapped, or abruptly ended a conversation or relationship or turned on someone after a seemingly uneventful meeting, think about what lines were crossed when all of these happened.

Think about whether you knew they were there in the first place and whether you realised they were being crossed in real time.

We all have places we do not want to go to, extents at which we break when we can bend no further. Fine. We had better know what, where, which, and when.

Wooly boundaries are as uncomfortable for other people as they are for us. For who likes to have their reverie of a quiet afternoon shattered by caterwauling or crying or otherwise a complete reversal of a picture they thought they knew so well.

Much better to draw your line in the sand. This is where we end and others begin and never the twain shall meet.

### Unrealistic expectations

"Manage expectations" has been a big buzzword for some time. How about managing our own?

This is not to say that we must take a dim view of everyone around us, but we must certainly take a realistic one.

If we are bitterly disappointed in someone's reaction or someone breaks our heart, odds are very good that we had unrealistic expectations.

Yes, sometimes we are deliberately led into expecting what the other person cannot deliver, but hopefully, by the end of this book, you would have attended to that problem.

For our purposes, if we hold and maintain self-sufficiency no matter how promising the situation and potential looks, we will automatically temper our own expectations.

### Others as props

The almost flip side of living vicariously is to look to others to provide our lives with meaning and direction.

Or to look to others for what we should do and what actions we should take.

This dawned on me as I waded through hours and hours of marketing seminars and materials.

There is a whole world of great information and good people out there, and Oh! how I wished someone would just take the decisions off my shoulders and do it all for me. And while this could happen, I still would have to make the decision of who that someone would be.

At the nearest degree of separation, I cannot abdicate that responsibility.

Similarly with our lives, when we are exhausted and overwhelmed it is reasonable to wish for or to lean on someone or something for a time, but not as a lifestyle or a way of being.

The habit of leaning on others might creep up on us gradually and is then uncovered at the most unexpected and inconvenient of times, so we must be on the alert.

To expect the people around us to order our existence in a manner that would best suit us would be the most unrealistic of all expectations. And more often than not results in a falling-out as the consequences are predictably not to our liking.

If we tell ourselves and each other that we are happy to be together that's a much better way of looking at it than that *they make us happy*. Nope. No props allowed.

# 4

## POLITICAL CORRECTNESS

"Looking for 'fat' Caucasian men to help promote a shopping mall. The right candidate has to be 'fat,' cheerful and be willing to have fun on the job."

This was taken from an actual advertisement on an online job site, which perturbed my husband greatly, which was how it came to light. Every adjective offended his every sense. I, however, saw absolutely nothing wrong with it. If they wanted a fat Caucasian male, why not ask for one, I reasoned.

We finally agreed that since we saw this in January, which had probably been posted in December, the advertiser had most likely wanted a Santa Claus-type figure, who we cannot but concede, is a fat Caucasian male! In between, of course, there was much discussion of the polite way to phrase these things, and also, should these requirements even be voiced given possible racial overtones.

The "politically correct" thing of nondiscrimination is really laughable. As is the nonspecification of gender, age, spiritual bias, whatever we humans like to peg our likes and dislikes on.

Because, guess what? No matter what is put in a job posting or what is not, choices will be made by the preferences of the interviewer. Regardless of how it is justified. And why not? They are the people who have to work with the successful candidate.

Let us be very clear, this is not an argument for discrimination. This is an argument against hiding discrimination that exists. Any kind of relationship that is sought on a basis other than merit it best done openly and if not, the consequence *will* be failure.

Why do we have politically correct forms of naming things anyway? African Americans, South Asians, Mentally Challenged — though I'm not too sure how politically correct that last is.

Ostensibly, it is to show respect or to not give offence: in the end it is "politic."

Here's a Merriam-Webster definition of politic: characterised by shrewdness in managing, contriving, or dealing.

It is a manipulation that is epic in its dishonesty. It oftentimes provides a cover and safe harbour for someone to hide their prejudices, lack of respect and understanding, and profound lack of willingness to rectify all of the above.

I completely agree that words have immense power; it is the reason I love reading and writing. Words and language should be used carefully, with due thought to the sensitivities of others as weighed against your own opinions. And there's the rub.

Behind the politically correct terms, who

knows what the politically incorrect opinions are? Like meaningless corporate catchphrases, they are repeated by rote; nobody questions anything, and all is smooth.

While some might argue that potentially nasty actions and deeds are nipped in the bud by being politically correct, I wonder at this.

Truth will out at some point. People will discriminate in action, if they discriminate in thought. They will be unjust and unfair if so inclined. They will be greedy and immoral if that is their leaning. You have only to look at the scandals in industry, politics, and religious houses to see the truth of this. The politically correct front and the morass (no pun intended) of wrongness it was hiding.

The most dire result of political correctness is the veil it draws over ugly reality.

At the end of the day, if we strip away trite terms, I can agree with the rationale of being politically correct — sensitivity and acceptance. But "sensitivity and acceptance" have no meaning if they do not actually exist.

In fact, it is much more damaging, because the offender cannot be called to book — they are squirreled away behind their shield of acceptable words and phrases, innocent till proven guilty.

So what does this leave us with? A seething underbelly of issues that cannot get addressed. A set of attitudes that do not see the light of day and are therefore exempt from criticism and reformation.

A culture of half-truths and lies that makes

someone feel like Alice down the rabbit hole.

I am reminded of a kerfuffle when I was younger. Someone accused me, complainingly, of spreading the tale of something that had happened involving both of us.

They obviously thought it did not reflect well on them, and therefore it was mean spirited of me to repeat it to others.

In actuality, I had done no such thing, being most disinclined to bruit about my own doings, never mind someone else's. I, in turn, was complaining to my Father about the cheek of them thinking me capable of such gossiping.

To which my Dad responded, completely missing the point, but providing me with an everlasting catchphrase nonetheless, saying, "You should ask them, 'Am I lying? You did or not?'" Translated from Anglo-Indian speak: did they in truth behave as was being spoken about or not?

Wonderfully succinct and forever more the lodestone of correctness.

Ultimately we will all have to stand up and be counted for what we believe and the actions we take. This is not a day of judgement scenario, but a living day to day experience of how our lives unfold. We cannot hide behind a politically correct façade without paying the piper at some point.

If you have to mask the answer to the questions — did you do it, think it, act it, mean it — behind prefabricated phrases, then "it" is perhaps something to be leery of and something to be corrected at its root.

If we intend to be "correct," and by all means,

let us be, let us not make it political. Let's be REALLY correct. Really respectful of race. Really not discriminate on gender, age, facial features, and position in life.

If we looked at one another with clear eyes, unclouded by learned or absorbed bias and prejudice and went forward on that basis, then we *will* be correct.

# REDEFINING TERMS

# 5

## JUDGEMENT

I've been talking to a number of very good and compassionate people recently, and the subject of judgement has come up several times. And how that is a really, really bad thing.

This comes about through a common misperception of and confusion between two things: having good judgement and sitting in judgement. The former is essential and the latter is pretty pointless.

When it comes to our lives it is critical to be able to gauge correctly and consistently what fits us and what is better dispensed with. If we do not do this or if we misjudge, we live our lives with a hodgepodge of bad choices that we try to make the best of. Not ideal.

Suffice it to say, I think we must judge, and in fact, we DO judge, whether we can admit it or not.

We are all taught in our politically correct world, that we shouldn't judge, or correct, or otherwise flag behaviour we think shouldn't happen. The reasons for this are many and varied, and I don't agree with most of them.

For example, we hesitate to judge either lest we be judged or we be accused of assuming the mantle of God.

There is also the notion, that unless we are purer than driven snow, we ought not to be pointing fingers or throwing stones within glass houses.

Fair enough.

Does that stop us?

Oh no! We judge away. From what brand of clothes, to physical appearance, to clothing size. From which school, to which college, to which company. From activities, to hobbies, to locality we live in.

We have the whole "first impressions" science down pat, which covers all the obvious externals. There are the more subtle ones like company title, wealth, relative position to ourselves, whether they know someone we like or dislike etc.

Make no mistake, judgements abound and are alive and well.

What would be good to consider, then, is what do we judge people on?

I would much rather see a world where we judge on real merit. The character and moral fibre of a person. Are they positive? Do they inspire us be the best we can be? Are their intentions good and pure? Do their values and principles match our own? And are these constructive or are they destructive?

In truth, it is absolutely critical for us to make judgements and to hone our skills of critical thinking. But this is not a judgement about right and wrong on a global basis, this is a judgement on what is right and wrong for us. And who is right or wrong for us.

The sooner we can size this up for ourselves, the faster we are able to get a feel for what nourishes us or what incapacitates us and the quicker and more accurately can we make the decisions about who we allow into our lives.

So how do we set about developing judgement or discernment or critical thinking?

We need a powerful sense of what we would like to have in our relationships and the kind of feeling we would like to be left with after any encounter.

For example: we would like our relationships to be free of drama and misunderstandings. We would like easy communication and never any cold silences or hissy fits. We would like to feel utterly satisfied and deeply contented after a meeting with friends, family or a day at the office.

We need to be clear as well about what we wouldn't like and the feelings we particularly want to avoid feeling.

For example: we don't want to have superficial, meaningless encounters and conversations. We don't want relationships we cannot rely on and that make us feel insecure. We don't want to feel unloved, disrespected, and undervalued.

It is crucial that you delve into the depths of your heart, find out and articulate exactly what you want out of your relationships and then judge, yes, judge all your current and future associations against these standards.

At the base of it, judgement is setting the standard for what you deem acceptable in your life and in your relationships. It will be well for you to set the bar very high.

So here we may have another reason why people might fear to judge. What if no one meets the standard? What if we are too picky?

Well then, it's back to taking stock and re-examining your values and goals for your life.

At the end of the day, if our standards for relationships are in line with who we are and where we are going in life, they will separate the wheat from the chaff nicely.

The people who will grace our lives will truly benefit and uplift us and be representative of all we hold dear. The rest will fall away as they should.

The very first step in building great relationships and an unblemished, joyful support network is to raise your ability to judge to wisdom.

What happens when we surround ourselves with people, situations, ideas, and beliefs that are healthy and joyful?

Magic!

Imagine life where every single interaction is fruitful, satisfying, profitable, helpful, nourishing. Joie de vivre, indeed. It all depends on what you allow into your life.

Judge well. Or as we used to say in the good old days — this is the fine art of discernment.

# 6

## FORGIVENESS

I have always had a beef with the Bible story of the Prodigal Son. For those of you who have not heard it, it goes like this.

A rich man had two sons. When the younger son reached his majority, he requested his father for his share of the inheritance, moved out of his father's house and proceeded to run through all his funds in whichever ways he saw fit. This course of action soon found him destitute and hungry and having to eat food from the tray of the pigs he was hired to look after.

In the midst of his misery, he recalled that his father's hired helpers lived much better than his current condition, so he resolved to return to his father's house and offer to be his hired help at the very least.

When his father saw and recognised him from a way off, his joy knew no bounds and he ordered clothes and food be prepared as befitted the son of the house. He welcomed him with warmth and love and the return of the Prodigal Son was celebrated with all the wealth and pomp at the father's disposal.

The elder son who had remained and was dutiful was most put out at the proceedings. He had never been feted thus and complained as much to his father. The father replied that there was much to celebrate in one who was lost being found.

Now, that's the essence of the story.

A great deal of emphasis has traditionally been placed on the mercy and forgiveness of the father. Such that forgiveness has been cast as the almightiest of virtues, the lack of which must surely blacken the soul of any transgressor.

My take is a little bit different. I focus on the remorse and humility of the son to admit his fault and return with the lowest expectations and no feelings of entitlement. The act and nature of his return made his welcome warm and loving.

I also have the greatest sympathy for the elder son and think it a bad object lesson that duty and doing what is right is taken for granted and not celebrated, while causing a ruckus and being regretful is. It's all of a piece!

The upshot of all of this is that forgiving has become one of the most overrated and misrepresented acts of our lifetime. The themes of forgiveness, remorse, and second chances are so twisted and convoluted that they are applied or withheld in haphazard and arbitrary ways that are painful to watch.

There is a lot of unnecessary burden and repeated grief associated with all of this.

As a result, we are expected to forgive those who hurt us. We are expected to encompass people who don't mean us well. We are expected to show mercy and understanding for egregious wrongs.

From another perspective, the notion of forgiveness implies a power to make things right by conferring this "blessing" for a wrong done to us. This is clearly illogical if the perpetrator is not only not contrite, but ready, willing, and able to hurt us again. This is when this delicate pack of cards comes tumbling down.

Our systems of justice swing wildly between each pole of this philosophy, such that there is no true progress or avenue for rehabilitation.

Nor is retribution an adequate answer or any answer, in the wider scheme of things. So what recourse do we have for healthy human engagement?

Starting with ourselves, the main argument put forward for forgiveness is to remove hate from our hearts. And this is the only sound premise in the lot of this.

For this is true.

Vengeance, hate, and anger only serve to bring our own energies down, while doing precious little damage to the objects of these. If we choose to act on any of these feelings, we may do damage to our targets, but make no mistake, we do even more damage to ourselves. In the material and physical sense of suffering, by the consequences that might be meted out in society, but more so, in the psychic sense of kicking ourselves further away from the path of evolution.

At the same time, there is no logic to or reason for accepting hurtful behaviour or words over and over again. We must let the people around us know in no uncertain terms that there are levels of relating that we will not tolerate.

I have a better solution.

*Acceptance.*

We merely have to view unacceptable acts in the cold light of day and as they are without excuses. Then we have to accept what they mean. At the very root of it, painful experiences and relationships in which pain far outweighs rewards and joys are symptomatic of one thing: a lack of caring. This is what we must accept.

Depending on the degree of discomfort, we can gauge how cared for we feel. We must realise that we have no control over how people feel about us. The way they act is a reality and is the next thing we must accept.

And finally, we have to look within ourselves and see what it is we are willing to put up with. How far are we willing to bend, how many allowances are we willing to make. If we are pushed beyond our limits, we must end the relationship and possibly avoid the person or any such situation again. That is the final acceptance.

There are no blessings to be had in forgiving people who mean us ill. There are many blessings attached to accepting that they do, accepting them for what they are, and taking every step to make sure we are safe from harm.

So what happens when the boot is on the other foot? When we are the people asking or seeking forgiveness?

It behooves us to admit our error and really examine why we acted or spoke as we did.

It might well be a profound lack of caring for the person or thing. In which case, own it, release the relationship, and let sleeping dogs lie.

On the other hand, if it points to a situation that needs remedying or significant change that is within our power and inclination to make, take the appropriate action wholeheartedly.

If you are genuinely remorseful and ready to do what it takes to not have the incident or experience repeat, then that will show itself and time will heal all wounds.

Repentance, forgiveness, and absolution are intrinsically bound up with each other. Ultimately, there can be no absolution from an external source. The only absolution you can meaningfully achieve is from yourself.

Likewise, it is not in our power to "forgive" or "absolve." The forces that truly heal relationships are, and should be, only generated organically and mutually between the people concerned.

What is in our power is to remove any trace of negativity or bias within ourselves and create situations in which we are not at the receiving end of behaviors that would require "forgiveness."

Bottom line: it benefits no one to be in a repeated cycle of offense and forgiveness. It is harmful in the extreme as hurt and pain must have an outlet, even if it's inward, and will destroy us according to the magnitude of the grief.

The best scenario is one in which you have no need for hate, anger, or vengeance and your relationships are inoculated from pain by acceptance and avoidance.

# 1

## LOVE

A very cathartic song is Tina Turner's "What's Love Got to Do with It." An outcry against the social requirement of slapping the term "love" over the reason for being in a relationship.

But it's not just the concept of romantic love that serves as an umbrella, sheltering all manner of motives and agendas that operate quietly in the background.

As mentioned in *Going Home*, we have lost perspective on what it means to truly love and be loved. We only know this in the negative. We know when we are not loved or do not love, all the rest is a morass of ifs and buts and unfortunate shades of grey.

Our misconceptions start and end with our eager expectations of "love." That we should love everyone. That we should be loved by everyone in turn. That when that happens, rainbows form in the sky, castles rise up from the ground, kids turn out perfectly in time for barbecues in the backyard, which is overflowing with warmth-exuding friends and family.

Reality might be a tad different and slightly more messy. And it is all because "love" may not be "love" at all.

What is certain is this: if you surround yourself by real love — filial, platonic and sexual — you will have all the rainbows, castles and barbecues your heart can desire.

Critical first step: you must be able to distinguish love.

Let us start by examining what it is not.

The most common masquerader of love is fear.

### Fear of being alone

Fear that we are some freak of nature who cannot be in a relationship, cannot have friends, that we are someone no one likes being around. So we hang on to our relationships like a lifeline.

We need to claim ownership so that we can feel secure and anchored in our relationships. Everyone around us becomes ours. We view with distrust new friends joining our social circle, offers of help, new horizons for our partners and friends. All of this signals to us that they may depart and we will be that dreaded thing — alone.

Love is not possessive or demanding. Something that this fear can give rise to.

The associations we have soothe our fear, we can push it to the backs of our mind, but it will never go away and we cannot really love until we get rid of this fear. Until we can stand on our own two feet and love from our own independence.

### Fear that we are not good parents, good relatives, good neighbours

This is from that "love everyone" program going on in our heads.

For whatever reason, if we feel somewhat less than "loving" towards the people around us, we redouble our efforts. We say we love them fifty times a day, we make every effort to do what is considered the caring things to do. We create a lovely facade of loving families, friends, and neighbours.

But it is not necessarily love.

### Fear of what society might say

This is keeping up with the Joneses in the worst possible way. We maintain our relationships based on how it looks on the outside.

Facebook is a good example of this kind of oneupmanship, where getting friends and likes can become a huge driver of interactions. Retaining relationships because they make us look good is certainly not love.

Those are but a few cuckoos in the nest of pure love, and there are many. The one infallible indicator of love is how it makes you feel. The most pressing reason to get in touch with your emotions.

If you feel unloved or unable to love, you can bet the farm that you are unloved or the object of your "love" is unworthy of it in some way. The real you under all those layers of musts and shoulds will know.

Anything other than love will manifest as sadness, loneliness, depression, rage, and a million other negatives, but never joy.

So how do we recognise love?

Love, when we are giving it or receiving it, is supremely energising. Of this it is true that the more we give, the more we can give. There is a joyful freedom in loving wholeheartedly without thought of gain, without fear of loss. It is a free resource shared out of never-ending abundance.

It is truth. It does not create scenarios that are soon proved false. It does not set people up on a pedestal. It does not use people as a crutch. It makes real the concept of warts and all, except the warts are not seen as warts, they are seen as an integral part of the people we love and it's all good.

Having said that, it includes a comprehensive non-caveat-ridden acceptance for people as they are. It is very freeing, the people around us are free to be and we are free from the burdens of trying to make them into an image of our liking.

It is discipline. Foremost of ourselves, to care enough to have consideration, to not take more than someone can give, to have the sensitivity to know how much that is. And towards others, to caution them when they are infringing our bounds in turn. The dance of holding integrity in relationships becomes effortless when it is done with love.

And finally the million dollar-question! But shouldn't we love everybody, shouldn't we love our enemies? Eckhart Tolle summed it up nicely in his answer, "have no enemies." This is brilliant in its simplicity and applicability.

What does that mean for us in this global village that we live in?

Very simply this: choose well.

There are people in this world you simply will not be able to love. It may or may not be a fault in them or you, but it is a fact that there are many attitudes, customs, and beliefs that are far removed from our own.

Perhaps a day will come when our spirits are wide enough and deep enough to encompass many universes, but until that time, don't fuss about loving all of peoplekind.

Instead, just focus on creating an inner circle of people you can truly and unreservedly love. Release the rest.

Voila! You have no enemies, and you love one another.

# 8

## EFFORT

I hope that by the end of this chapter, I will have blasted apart the myth in your mind that relationships should be worked at and require effort. If the last chapter had any effect, it should have started making inroads into this belief.

This is no doubt a result of the disservice done by the self-help industry in a bid to have us all have harmonious relationships.

At the risk of sounding facetious, the only way to having harmonious relationships is to have harmonious relationships. And not have conflicted relationships that we splice together by papering over the cracks with various techniques and changes to ourselves.

The idea we commonly have about relationships is that they cannot be perfect. There is always some adjustment required that oftentimes will be unpleasant and not exactly what we wanted to do, but there's no help for it.

Since we perceive it as absolutely necessary, we bend over backwards or at the very least are mildly discomfited by what we have to do to maintain our relationships.

As P.G. Wodehouse would have it, if we are not exactly disgruntled, we are far from being gruntled.

At the foundation of this is that we don't believe relationships can be effortless, and therefore, we don't look for ease in relationships, we don't make arrangements to make it so and we put up with what we have in the conviction that this is normal.

And we couldn't be more wrong.

The understanding we have of effort is an unusual exertion of ourselves, physically, emotionally, or otherwise to bring about some desired end. And this much is true. The other part of effort is strain, that it is okay for it to be unedifying, either mildly or acutely.

I put it to you, that you must be edified at all times while making an effort towards anything or anyone. Should this be your goal, you will find, everything becomes effortless. Your "effort" is sublimated in your joy or satisfaction, and it becomes no effort at all.

In a recent conversation, we were talking about this, where my idea of life being effortless was pulled into question.

The example we used was of learning a musical instrument – which requires, admittedly, a goodly amount of effort. However, if it is your burning desire to learn this instrument, then the hard work of doing so is put in willingly and industriously wherever and whenever you can fit it in.

In fact, effort at this level boosts you into the zone or flow of your consciousness and has exponential rewards for doing that.

Likewise, for any learning curve of things we *choose* to do and learn.

Another significant differential in effort is the direction in which it is exerted. If, for example, I really wanted someone as a business or romantic partner, but if through various actions and words I am assured that my intention is not reciprocated, then I have two options.

I could make a supreme effort to change the other person's mind or to change myself with a view to changing their minds. Or, if after weighing everything in the balance, I decided that the change required will not be beneficial to me, I can make the effort to rejig my own thinking and feeling in order to detach from my initial desire and level the playing field.

Both require effort. Both require changing someone towards doing something they don't want to do. We have a better chance of that with ourselves than with someone else. And quantifiably better odds for success.

When we are more used to developing relationships without the use of force, coercion, or manipulation, we will truly appreciate the importance of this. It is infinitely more satisfying when relationships come into being of their own volition and remain for the same reason.

The effort we put into making ourselves see and understand what's out there and who is naturally for us or not, not only allows us to have excellently flowing relationships, but it also boosts our understanding and confidence in ourselves.

We develop the ability to hold back, to not push people into associations they ultimately will back out of and to not create artificial scenarios brought about by our own overriding requirements.

If we approach relationships with this frame of mind, then the ebbs and flows of relating hold no monsters for us.

We become one with ourselves and the people around us. We have no need for pseudo-expressions of goodwill; we have no need for quasi-concerns. Genuine desire to be with our friends and family is the paramount and overarching sentiment.

It overrides differences of opinion, belief, and being. It makes all the adjustments for exquisite harmony all the more enjoyable and easy because it flows naturally, without effort.

Make no mistake, the relationships worth having are, and always will be, effortless.

# 9

## PAIN

We are a global society that is fixated on one thing — removal of pain. We shield ourselves from it as much as possible by hardening our hearts, avoiding looking too closely at anything that might prove to be remotely unsettling, and watching TV to help with all of this.

If all of the above fail, then we self-medicate in a frenzy with retail therapy, our favourite addiction, or actual medication.

This is a self-perpetuating system because we have lost track of the meaning of pain: it merely means that something is wrong and wants fixing.

If we don't allow ourselves to feel pain and examine it, how on earth are we going to fix it?

When we are physically wounded, we staunch any bleeding, we clean up the wound, we add healing ointments perhaps, and then we protect it till it heals. If we have something drastically wrong, like a tumour or a blockage, we rush to surgery and get it removed and monitored.

How much happier we would be if we took care of our emotional selves with such diligence.

I recently read *Good As New*, a flash fiction piece by Shane Rhinewald that is shockingly graphic in exactly this way to very good effect.

It tells of a young girl who comes back from school every day with an increasing number of holes in her person. An excellent portrayal of what we do to each other and allow to be done to ourselves.

The goal for most of us is to live our lives as pain free as possible, and that is quite a reasonable requirement as these things go.

It should not be confused with anesthetising ourselves against pain. We do this in innumerable ways — by shutting other people out, by adopting hard and fast attitudes that narrow our experience of life, by only accepting news, experiences, and relationships that conform to that narrow view of the world we hold and, in short, by constructing an artificial world for ourselves that we can control.

The problem is, reality has the unhappy knack of intruding at the worst possible time.

If we are in the very depths of make-believe, it takes a tragedy of awful magnitude to unlock us from this fixed universe and then the consequences to us are severe.

Think this is not true? We see stories in the news all the time, of extreme reactions to changes in fortune and status. Those are the signs of a universe crumbling.

Or we simply don't think about it — the ostrich method. We bury our heads in the sand in the futile hope that when we surface for air, the problem would have gone away, people would have miraculously changed and we can carry on in our mutinous belief that all is well.

There is an old story of a town that was peopled by very, very good people. They had no sin, no crime, and no temptations. Their lives were serene and untrammeled by evil.

The devil took a bet that he could corrupt the town in no time at all. And he won. Because the townspeople had no experience of and no immunity to evil.

Substitute good in that story with pain-free and pain will take you over with similar ease if you've been ducking and diving to avoid it.

The way I look at it, we have a choice. It is between the pain of denial and the pain of growth. Both have some possible discomfort associated with it. The biggest difference is that the former is unending, and the latter ends the minute you grow out of it.

Now which would you choose?

The latter? Excellent!

Let's leave the pain of denial behind and take a look at what growing pains look like.

It requires us to shed our blinkers or blinders and take a good look at who is around us. How do we feel after an interaction with them? Do we feel loved, cherished, secure?

If we don't, why not? Are we too needy, are we asking too much? Are we insecure within ourselves to start off with?

Do we need something from our relationships that we cannot get? In other words, the person or persons do not have the capacity to fulfill us. Maybe the schism is too wide and deep to be bridged.

What are your intentions towards each other? Do you actually love each other? Do you mean well by each other and want the best for the other person?

These are hard questions. They are even harder when they must be answered by the raw truth.

And here you have the pain of growth.

If you can face the reality of all your relationships squarely, take the hit for the ones that are under par and then do something about it, you will find you can breathe through the pain and come out the other end with something infinitely more valuable: a set of relationships that are profoundly meaningful.

And surprise, surprise: pain-free! In the best of all possible ways, because you have come *through* the pain, struggle, and confusion instead of skirting around it.

# CHOICES

# 10

# CALIBRE OF ASSOCIATIONS

"The road to hell is paved with good intentions."

Even though I use this myself and have used it in the past when it hit the nail on the head, sitting here now thinking of intentions, I cannot see how it is possible.

If you intend to do good, how does that lead to hell? And yet, we see actions that are "good" on the surface meeting with hellish consequences.

While good and hell are constructs that are contentious in the infinite variations of their interpretation, let's leave them for the moment, to deal with intentions.

From Merriam-Webster: *intention: the thing that you plan to do or achieve : an aim or purpose* which implies little more than what one has in mind to do or bring about; *intent: the state of mind with which an act is done* which suggests clearer formulation or greater deliberateness.

It's funny to me how, by definition and understanding, the former can be such a diluted wash of the latter. By what degree of determination is: "I have every intention of doing xyz" different from "I intend to do xyz." Something to think about.

So let us discuss intent, I think this is what guides ultimate outcomes. Because depend upon it, nine times out of ten, what you intend to happen, will happen. It's the law of the universe and the power of the mind.

Critically important when it comes to relationships is to have your intent be congruent with your spoken intention. Likewise, to surround yourself with people who are similarly congruent.

The inescapable fact is that people know, even if only on a subliminal level, whether what you are saying or doing is for the right reasons, or at a basic level, for their benefit or detriment. And the effectiveness of your actions will be impacted by this as well — by cooperation or revolt or simply no result at all.

And whether they can put their finger on it or not, most people are aware of a disconnect when what they see is not the feeling of what they are getting.

Have you ever been with people who are polite, even charming, but you feel unsettled, despondent, just downright not quite right? Or someone does something that, on the surface, seems very good, but the final outcome is at odds with their stated intentions? Or the reverse when someone seems harsh but you feel kindness and caring? And sometimes there is truth and love behind being cruel to be kind.

Have you ever come across people who say: "I really want to help you" and then they either disappear, or are neutral or, worst of all, prove to be a hindrance? What did they actually intend?

The converse is also equally valid — where someone does something apparently radical, against conventional wisdom, disapproved of by many, but the outcome is glorious in its splendour and positivity. History is full of them. And also the other sort.

We all have inexplicable sensations or experiences like these, and without question, the intangible factor is intent. Do these people have good or bad intent?

Does this mean that we all have to be do-gooders? No. Most assuredly not. It just means that if you are not a do-gooder, stand up and be counted as such!

From the point of view of smoothing our path in life, it behooves us to look for and understand the intent of a person, no matter what they are promising us.

The insidiousness of overt "good intentions" then, is that it masks everything from disinterest to malice. That is a dangerous thing. In our interactions with others, we need to be very clear in our souls what it is we intend and what do others intend for us.

This requires sometimes a deep analysis — starting with our own lives and purpose. What do we intend for ourselves, do we intend anything for who we are, what we will become and where we will end up? Or are we living unexamined lives, blowing in the wind like dandelion wisps.

Once we've formulated that, we need to question carefully what we intend in our dealings with others.

Not just for their benefit, though it would be nice if we all started passing some consideration around, but ours. Our own credibility, reputation, and efficacy depend on it.

True intent as with everything that is actual, has the immense power of reality a.k.a. truth behind it — for better or for worse.

From an outward point of view, therefore, you need to examine also the intent of others. Do their words and actions impact you positively or negatively?

And right here for me, is the crux of divining true intent. It is to not accept bad intent, to call people on the inconsistencies of their behaviour and speech. At a very minimum, to not allow bad intent or anything less than best wishes into our lives.

How does evil continue to exist and go unpunished?

It is with collusion from all of us.

We respond with:

Blinkers or blinders

Excuses

Acceptance

Apathy

Ignorance

Blindness

Time to shake these off. Look to ourselves and look to others.

If you see your world or the world at large heading to Hades in a hand basket, which increasingly it seems to be, without a doubt, somebody, somewhere intends it to be so.

In which case, start looking in your neighbourhoods, work, social circles, and family circles, and weed toxicity out of your life.

### Three energies

If you are in the least bit psychically aware, you will be conscious of vibrations or energy emanating from people. Even if you are unconscious of this, there are people that you are automatically drawn to and people who repel you.

This is not a figment of your imagination. Though it may be a result of conditioning or superficial judgements.

It is imperative that you clear your own internal space and develop your Core of Steel sooner rather than later, because this sensing of energies is critical to finding and forming meaningful and uplifting relationships.

To get right down to it, there are three energies you could receive from people. Funnily enough, they are positive, neutral, and negative.

The distinction here is that these are energies, not people. You could have a "negative" or gloomy person who gives you positive energy; you could have a "positive" person give you neutral energy, etc. It's a very subjective experience of course, because these are energies directed at you, personally.

### Positive

When you are on the receiving end of positive energies, the "Good Vibrations" of the Beach Boys, you leave every encounter deeply satisfied.

There is nothing you could say or do that would mar the good feeling between all parties.

There is a sense of nourishment, like a drink of water on a hot day, the sense like some deep part of you has been replenished. These same energies apply to advice you receive, books you read, movies you watch, and places you visit. Some of them will have a richness of quality that enriches you in turn.

### Neutral

Some of our associations are sum neutral. We can take them or leave them, they can take us or leave us — they're either pleasant enough or not sufficiently unpleasant to stir great emotion in us either way.

Most of our casual acquaintances and chance-met people in our lives who remain so have this kind of energy.

### Negative

Boy, do you know it when you are on the receiving end of negative energy.

This manifests as unhelpful, rude, cruel, mocking, bullying, and every single damaging behaviour you can think of. And that's if you are lucky. We instinctively avoid people who are overtly negative and hurtful.

The thing to be on full alert for are the covertly negative energies. This could manifest as smiling faces, expressions of concern and love, but you leave every encounter feeling drained, depleted, and in some indefinable way, diminished.

If you are not fully aware of what and who energises you or makes you tired, I urge you to start paying attention.

If we go through life on auto-pilot, we cannot mark the relationships that bring us our greatest joys and why, or flag the things that create our greatest griefs and why. We will not be able to remedy the latter and accentuate the former if we are not conscious of the differences. Call it gut instinct, call it intuition, but just develop it in a hurry.

And then do not ever dismiss the feelings people leave you with. Examine it from a "me or them" perspective, but when it comes to negative energies, it is better to remove yourself from that circle of influence in the first instance.

When you are aware of the energies you receive from the people around you, separate them into these three categories and now you have the basis for making informed decisions about the relationships in your life.

# 11

## REALITY CHECK

In the light of how nourished you are by your relationships, take a look at every single one of them. How do you feel overall? Cheered right up? Or frightened to the core?

If all your relationships satisfy you on some level, then that is an excellent indication that you have either consciously or unconsciously been paying attention to who you truly are. If you expand that out and extrapolate it to your daily life, situations, and the world around you, you will be more than halfway to your dream life.

There is a joke about a polite curator, who could not bring himself to criticize anything. He was given a rotten egg for breakfast by mistake (we hope) and upon being asked how he found his egg he replied "Oh! It's good in parts."

If your relationships are like the polite curator's egg — good in parts and bad in parts, but generally rotten, then it's time to do a reality check and weed out behaviours that run counter to your health requirements.

If the behaviours can't go, then maybe their owners should. These are the choices before you and ones you must make in the near future before you proceed further with your life.

This is an essential skill in life, to clear house, to get rid of detritus and redundancies in order to make way for the fresh and the new. Admittedly, we very rarely apply this to people as this is considered a very non-pc thing to do.

Well, my opinion of pc has been made manifestly clear, so I will reiterate, the people in your life who are harming you must go. End of story.

If you have any doubts, try to take a deep breath without exhaling. I did it once in a yoga class upon the instruction to inhale after I had just inhaled without thinking about it. I almost burst a blood vessel! Ever so slightly difficult.

I have since done very vigorous and thorough exhales before inhaling and then, bliss and joy, clean and clear air fills up my lungs. It's a fantastically satisfying feeling.

So it is with relationships. If even a breath of unease remains, it will affect your energy and hobble your ability to form new and productive bonds. It's like a tendril of gravity that holds you back, you need to boost yourself away from it.

### Vacuums

Do not fear vacuums, they are responsible, after all, for relieving you of earthly weight. If you find the better part of your associations must go, do not grieve. Or if you must, get real about what you are grieving for.

Odds are good that you are grieving the death of your own illusions. The illusion that you were loved and happy and had the perfect life.

No matter that there were niggling doubts and periods of sorrow that made you question it in the first place.

The vacuum always existed, the difference is now you acknowledge it to be so. And that can never, ever be a bad thing.

However unpleasant reality is, the incontrovertible fact is that it is reality. When, and only when, you can accept it with all its drawbacks, can you begin to shift it to what you want.

The shift begins with releasing what you don't want.

Go ahead! Create that vacuum with impunity.

Be comforted with this thought: You cannot lose what is real, no way, not in this lifetime, not ever. What does that mean in practicalities? If you lose something, it was not real.

If relationships change, then that's what they have to do, and if you allow it to run its course, it will settle as it should. At which point you can make this assessment again on a fresh new set of parameters.

And if you have doubts but still release relationships, the true ones will come back to you. Proof positive that they are real, based in genuine emotion and deep connections.

This is admirably expressed in this quote from Richard Bach's *Jonathon Livingston Seagull*, "Don't be dismayed at goodbyes, a farewell is necessary before you can meet again and meeting again, after moments or lifetimes, is certain for those who are friends."

The important thing is to allow time and space between you, time and distance to affect and assess change and the inevitable result. Allow yourself time and space to consider what you might have lost and gained and appreciate them both.

And when you have some distance and perspective, only then consider what you would like in your life. Nature will rush to fill a vacuum, it does not have to be so with you. Hold your space until people of the calibre you wish for cross your path.

What we call mental health is sufficiency, as a minimum, at all levels. Your first responsibility to yourself, then, is to make yourself invulnerable to desperate choices by establishing this at the earliest opportunity.

The best relationships are born of independence, which at the end of this exercise will be hard won, so cherish it and yourself. Then you won't *have* to have people cherish you, but you will find you will get that anyway. Simply because you will not settle for less.

# 12

## FUNDAMENTAL FIXES

In Chapter 10, we looked at the three different types of energy at work in our relationships: positive, neutral, and negative. It will benefit you greatly at this point if you create three lists of the types of relationships in your life: the good, the bad, and the ugly.

The good, comprised of the positive and nourishing relationships, stay.

The bad, comprised of the negative, those relationships that have no redeeming features, are out.

The ugly, comprised of conflicted relationships, which may have no redeeming features but necessity or circumstance does not allow you to cut them off...need work.

It bears reminding at this point, that relationships are not meant to be sources of hard labour. They are meant to be holiday resorts, not prison camps.

So I will make the assumption that the relationships you choose to work on are with people who might be a mite totty-headed, or exhibit flawed judgement from time to time, but are essentially good-hearted and hold your best interests dear or may not be as good-hearted as you might like, but need you in some essential way.

Be that as it may, there is one demonstrably sound basis for relationships. It is this: everyone must and will act in their own self-interest.

You may try to wheedle around it, play martyr, victim, or dictator, but this is so. And a good thing too, once a healthy sense of self-interest is developed.

What this means for relationships is simply this. You only have a viable relationship if your self-interests coincide *or* if you make it your self-interest to nourish the other person and vice versa.

Make no mistake. Any other combination will ultimately fail or result in one or two very deeply damaged people.

Take for instance, someone who acquiesces to all the demands put on them by their friends and relatives with little regard for their own needs and inner sustenance. At some point, they will either explode or, what is less healthy, go into depression or have a nervous breakdown.

If you can take this as read, it makes navigating relationships a whole lot easier. There are no ifs and buts, the people around you either uplift you and help you as a person or they don't. Likewise for yourself; you can be of assistance and have the satisfaction of helping your friends or not.

And when the give and take of relationships is balanced out to everyone's satisfaction, you have relationships in harmony.

With that in mind, back to our less than satisfactory but have immense potential relationships. What do we do?

We must highlight and isolate what it is exactly we find objectionable and decide for ourselves whether is it justified. Remember the self-interest thing. If it is reasonable to ask for change, then that's what we must do, but we cannot demand.

There are three distinct but equally effective techniques for effecting change.

### Disarm

I just had a happy memory of a very good and extremely funny example of a request for change.

As with all good stories, it starts a very long time ago in India. We used to be supplied milk by a milkman who would come around with a large barrel of milk on the back of his bicycle.

On his resonating bellow at some unearthly hour of the morning, whoever was unfortunate enough to be awake at that time, would stagger out with a pan into which he would transfer the required litres of milk using his one-litre measuring cup.

This agreeable arrangement had been going on for several months or maybe even years, until inexplicably, the milk starting going bad. This happened several days in a row.

My Dad after some thought came to the conclusion that the milkman was diluting the milk with dodgy water and so decided to tackle this head on.

He roused himself nobly the next morning and lay in wait for the hapless milkman. After the first litre of milk had been poured, my Dad bounded into view and said "Stop! Wait! Don't pour your water into the milk, just give it back to me and I'll put my clean water into it."

In vain did the milkman protest his innocence, only to be reassured soothingly by my Father in tones of compassionate kindness that he understood perfectly and sympathised. The man had only two cows, but now his customer base had doubled; he had to bridge the gap somehow...

And seeing as how that was, my Father would *much* prefer adding clean water to the milk, so that it wouldn't go bad.

"No sir, no sir," the poor man rigourously denied, while we were doubled up indoors at my father's voice of sweet reason.

Finally, he was permitted grudgingly to give us our full quota of milk and shot off with dispatch.

The milk never went bad after that, though. And I still laugh when I think of that scene.

A lesson in disarming with flair.

### Discourage

Sometimes, more stringent measures are required, where we simply state that this will never do, can something be done about it. Or simply to say this is how we feel about the relationship and our experience and it's not acceptable. The whole aim being to actively discourage things we cannot accept.

Discouragement requires us to not smile and/or agree to words and actions that we find disagreeable. It requires us to remove the façade of politeness we have been conditioned to wear and come out with the simple fact of our disapproval.

At the very least, the perpetrator of these disagreeable acts should be left with every conviction that we are not amused.

### Hold still

We could also, and this is usually the best way, hold firm to our convictions and life path and bring about change in others simply by being. And by not being swayed by any of their shenanigans.

This, of course, requires us to know what our convictions are. And to hold ourselves to our standards.

In this instance, we do not cajole or remonstrate, we continue our lives as we see fit and choose not to be derailed or disheartened by the relationships that are not working. If they fall into line that is all to the good, and if not they will be shed naturally and organically.

Whichever of these three change agents you use, it is important to keep in mind that how and when relationships change is not in your control.

You must, however, hold on tenaciously to the vision of how you want your relationships to be and monitor them from that perspective.

The ones that remain unsatisfactory and hurtful have to be let go, even if you are extremely reluctant to do so.

It is well to remember that you are letting it go in its current harmful-to-you form. If there is a real and enduring connection it will come back to you, changed and improved.

# 13

## FLAG RAISING

A few years ago, there was a kerfuffle in the news over a restaurant bill. A pastor took great exception to an automatic eighteen percent that had been added to the bill, scratched it out, and reduced it to zero. In addition and by way of explanation, something along the lines of giving God only ten percent, so eighteen percent to the server was questionable, was scrawled at the bottom.

It made the news when another employee of the restaurant uploaded a picture of the receipt, and it caught the attention and censure of the internet community.

To compound the problem, the pastor then called the restaurant to complain, which got the uploading employee fired and created even more outcry and grist to this particular mill.

What was most interesting in this little fiasco was that the pastor was outraged by the publicity and unwanted notoriety and declared that this incident, and therefore this employee, had caused embarrassment and ruination of reputation and standing.

What was most heartening was the almost complete consensus in the comments section of the article. Everyone was unanimous in the opinion that it was the pastor's actions alone that were cause for embarrassment. And therefore, the loss of reputation was not only completely justified, but inevitable.

There were so many points for redemption along the way of this short tale, and yet, none were taken.

For instance, not to do this to an establishment or person in the first place. Then maybe not to evoke God and your position and especially not when your actions are running counter to said God and position.

Then when outed maybe have the grace to be apologetic and remorseful, instead of putting the blame of your ignominy on the whistleblower.

From the restaurant's point of view, maybe weigh the magnitude of offense against the magnitude of punishment before taking action, which giving all of the foregoing resulted in a diminished reputation for them as well.

So, at the end of a few days, everybody lost. The pastor lost face, the waitress lost her job, and the restaurant lost customers and good faith. And it all started with one person.

But in a world where egregious miscarriages of justice are rife and bad behaviour goes all lengths from rudeness to mass murder, we must wonder why such actions and inclinations were not caught and stamped out at their infancy.

Surely someone around the people who cause madness and mayhem must notice something not quite right, or not ringing true?

Every instance of human tragedy and human misery has behind it a string of lost opportunities to correct minor wrongs and falsehoods and make them right before they erupt into crises that are inevitable.

Going forward, we must all overcome our resistance to raising flags. This is on both fronts: the first is flagging unreasonable behaviour in others, and the second, to continue the metaphor, is nailing our colours to the mast.

### Flag bad behaviour

There seems to be a global conspiracy at work to not flag people and attitudes that are manifestly out of order. We might wince at off-colour jokes and stare at some outlandish sentiment, but we will gamely laugh at the first and smooth over the second.

If we are to reorder our communications, which is critical, if we are to revamp our relationships, we must start out as we mean to go on. We must engage with people honestly.

We read horrendous stories of the rape and murder of women. School shootings. The downfall of prominent figures through cheating or crime. And we think these things are far away, they cannot touch us or the people we know. Ten to one, so did everyone involved in all the tragedies we see.

Without question, every little thing builds on itself. If you witness or experience destructive behaviour in the people you know, you must disregard your conditioned response and flag it.

And you must ensure your own safety while you do. Sometimes a flag could be the act of stepping away without excuses. Just do it.

If we hear friends and family speak ill of a group of people, be it gender, race, or creed, flag it. It is untrue and potentially harmful. Another of my favourite sayings: He who likes to generalise, generally lies.

If we see behaviour that raises our hackles, we must take action and the quicker it is taken the more effective it is, with less damage control needed.

The following example still gives me chills and serves to remind all of us how quickly a situation can go south.

It happened when I was in college and it was in the first few days of a new college year. Ragging or hazing, a practice I can never agree with incidentally, was rife and for the most part good natured. When all of a sudden, one of the new girls was thrown down in the middle of a circle of seniors and the mood turned ugly.

Without stopping to think, I jumped in, turned on the ring of seniors and demanded to know what they were thinking. In a second, the ring dissolved, I helped the new girl up and beat a hasty retreat.

These were not bad people and to this day, I don't know what happened. But there must have been a seed of bad energy somewhere that we did not pay attention to.

It is a poor reflection on our species that we can be so easily swayed to mayhem and misdeeds.

But it is so. And we must be on guard for it and stop it in its tracks at the earliest opportunity.

It is the classic case of one bad apple. I doubt the gangs of rapists and murderers that terrorise the planet are comprised unremittingly of evil people.

Some of them, I would hope, if removed from their peers might be horrified at what they have done. That does not mitigate anything, but what if they had been flagged and separated before the mob mentality took over. Might their victims still be alive?

Certainly, in the case of repeat offenders, there is no excuse for not taking action. For child molesters, for domestic violence, for exploitation of minorities. If it is in our immediate sphere, we must show by our words and actions that such a thing cannot be tolerated.

Ultimately, this is our responsibility to ourselves and our fellow human beings, for everyone's sake.

### Nailing our colours

We must never shy away from what we believe in and from requiring respect for those beliefs.

We hesitate to speak up in case our principles are not hip enough or we are too square or we are party poopers. For my part, if it's a destructive party, I am delighted to be a party pooper.

There is no shame in standing up for what is right. There is no question about standing up for someone who cannot defend themselves.

And it all begins with developing spines to stand up for ourselves.

We do not need the whole world to love us. We do not need to be the most popular people on the block.

We, as our true selves are powerful and stable beings. If we stand firm as who we are, the people who are good for us, who appreciate what we stand for will we drawn to us and will stay.

And that is how it should be.

# 14

## NOTE TO SELF

You cannot be in a relationship with a dishonest person. This is an immutable law. If any of the people around you are dishonest, you've got to ask yourself, who exactly is it you are having a relationship with? Again, this applies to all relationships, including a utility repairman.

If you cannot depend utterly on the people around you to do what they say they will, well, what's the point of hearing what they are saying? They are merely empty words in empty space.

So note to self. Create a network of people around you that you can trust one hundred percent.

And if as you read this you are thinking "Yes that's a nice idea, but what if... "

No ifs and buts. Look at it this way, no matter what someone promises you, if they cannot fulfill it, it is worthless. Period. Even if the picture they paint is everything you most want in life. Especially so, actually, because then your disappointment will be bitter indeed.

It is better to build self-reliance in the first instance and identify the people in whom you can place your trust, before handing over your heart, your confidences, your business and your life.

If you can establish trustworthiness as the core foundation of all your relationship requirements, I will guarantee you will never again be hurt, disappointed or ruined financially. It becomes impossible. You have made it so.

So what do you deserve to be surrounded by?

### Reliability

People you can count on.

People who step up to the plate when you need help, in fact, who might anticipate that you need help and provide it willingly.

People who do what they say, and if for some reason, they have to renege, tell you so in good time and maybe help you make other arrangements.

People for whom punctuality is not a movable feast and for whom deadlines and showing up on time are held sacred.

People who when you think about them bring a warm glow of safety and security. You are secure, they have your back, and you have theirs.

### Consistency

A close cousin of reliability, consistency perpetuates the feeling of constancy and security.

Consistency in terms of enduring affection and stability of actions and feelings creates relationships with deeper bonds, which are not subject to the whims of the moment.

This brings an über stable base of support that is very grounding in the swings and roundabouts of life.

To know that no matter how much time has passed, the core people in your life will not change or will change with you is a consummation devoutly to be wished. These kind of core connections just get deeper, stronger, and better with the passage of time.

### Consideration

This is the currency of give and take and the polar opposite of demanding without thought for the capacity of others.

It is of immeasurable value to have people around you that stop to consider your needs and balance them with their own and your collective life direction.

This gives rise to an effortless ecosystem of being, where needs are expressed and met on the basis of what works best for all parties.

Consideration keeps a constant eye on the other side of the coin and counterbalances an oversupply of "me first."

In doing so, it makes going the extra mile for ourselves and others a pleasure, because we know our needs have also been weighed up and accounted for.

### Curiousity

It is uplifting to associate with people who are curious about life. Who have an open mind. They are willing to learn more, do more, and help you do the same.

Curiousity never takes knowledge for granted and questions and deciphers everything in life.

This is not only interesting to watch and listen to, but expands the mind and expands our understanding of each other.

No matter what the subject matter is, it is deeply satisfying to discuss things with what is called "a beginner mind" in Buddhism.

When you are surrounded by curious people, somehow mundane issues of life are brought to meaningful light. Current events take on more than just a superficial reporting and communication becomes more than words, it can transmit a universe of comprehension.

### Proactiveness

Surround yourself with people who are willing to take life by the horns. They don't sit around and bemoan fate. They take fate and do a little jig with it. They make their own destiny.

They are able to gauge what will work, who will work, and thus are able to buffer against the slings of misfortune should it hit, but very often escape misfortune altogether by taking preemptive action.

### Accountability

It is an undiluted joy in life to be surrounded by people who can stand up and be counted for what they did or didn't do.

Who are responsible and diligent enough to take their medicine when they have made a mistake or fallen short.

Who can apologise with sincerity and make amends.

Accountability alone can sometimes make up for faults and flaws because it presents an attitude of attention and willingness to learn that is more compelling than any superficial charm and understanding.

### Caring

This is an absolute.

There are varying degrees of love and liking. Varying degrees of connection. The lowest-common denominator is caring.

Caring people make the world go 'round. They are the ones who give up their seat for a person in greater need, the ones who open doors, literally and figuratively. They have helping attitudes that are unblemished by ulterior motives, willing to help in any way, even if only by a smile and cheery greeting.

People who care exude an aura of joy and possibilities because who cannot be buoyed up by the feeling of being cared for? Learn how this feels, embed it in your DNA, and don't settle for less.

These are the characteristics of constructive and solid progress, and it is extremely critical to establish this as an environment around you.

What is important is to develop the discernment to distinguish for yourself the people who can fulfill all these characteristics for you, and cherish and nourish them in the same way, as is fitting.

# WRAPPING UP

# 15

# DON'T RATION PASSION

Like Pavlov's dog, we have all been conditioned to hogtie our responses. Between being once-bitten twice-shy and the social mores imposed on us by society and tradition, we are all but automatons, fearing honest emotion and fearing to give rein to all we feel.

But life is meant to be lived fulsomely, we are meant to live with passion, with all our senses, with all our might.

And therein lies the significance of choosing wisely and carefully who surrounds you.

Imagine this. If you are true to yourself, and you are surrounded by true relationships as reflected in these past pages, there is no side of yourself that you cannot try out and no evolution of any relationship that can be harmful.

It is all cushioned and cocooned in the incubator of genuine caring and concern and the strength of everyone as individuals. Not props, not crutches.

There is no neediness to cause fear, clutching, and limitation of individual growth. There are no insecurities that would be the prompt to bring someone else down. No jealousies or fears about success.

No there will be joy and celebrations. Freedom to grow and live. Freedom to have distance or not. Because the ties between you are not the ties that bind, just ties that support.

In this happy medium, you are free to cut loose and live your life to the fullest. To be who you are, to discover what else you can be. To dance all night, to sing at the top of your voice. To learn a new skill, to teach a new skill.

The merits of fulfilling associations cannot be stressed enough. And it can be used as a gauge of your current associations.

If you are hemmed in and discouraged from using all the talents and abilities available to you. If you are not even able to express what is in your heart and your dreams. Then you must reconsider who you want around you.

It may be that their dreams are not your dreams. That their limits on themselves are limiting you.

Someone I knew used to say this "How can I soar like an eagle when I'm surrounded by turkeys," that would unfailingly make me laugh just because it sounds so comical, but personal responsibility and endeavour aside, it is exponentially more difficult to make headway in life if the people around you are dragging you down.

If you feel an upward tug towards achievement and joy, you are better off responding to it and moving towards it. The worthwhile relationships will follow suit, and you might well become that proverbial rising tide that lifts all boats.

From a planetary perspective, this upward trajectory towards joy and peace is not only recommended, it is essential.

Create relationships that do not require you to ration passion. Instill in every encounter, every ounce of energy and attention that is you. What we need in society are scores of warm voices crying Hallelujah.

# 16

## ABOVE AND BEYOND

Along with living with passion, we ought to kick "duty" to the curb. If you are in a relationship in which you are "dutiful," odds are very good that you are also resentful. Is this necessary?

This is not to say that we should shirk our responsibilities. Precisely the opposite. We must evolve our relationships to the level where duty does not figure into the equation. It is far better to care for each other enough to do what needs to get done out of the sheer pleasure of doing it.

The whole concept of effortless relationships is predicated on not being dutiful.

Duty is a pale substitute for real love, caring, and a genuine desire to make things better. The case in point here is our relationships.

And when we perform the activities of relating on auto-pilot or under duress, we become the victims of a whole string of unconsciously intended consequences because "duty" alone can be very misguided and definitely blinkered. It can misdirect us in the worst ways.

The performance of duty per se, also has connotations of the minimum required effort to achieve a result. A perfunctory execution of relationship requirements, based on a label.

This performance of duty can be seen alive and well over holidays and family get togethers, for example. Or at all the big occasions of our lives, when we grit our teeth and invite people we do not want to.

So what is an alternative? So what should we be if not bound by duty?

Engaged.

In another lifetime, when I was a flight attendant, I was on a flight with an immensely lazy person, who happened to be the other flight attendant. It was a very short flight, which highlighted the extent of her laziness even more.

I cannot remember the exact number, but let's say of the sixty-five rows of passengers we both needed to serve, she did three, while I did sixty-two. This is not an exaggeration.

I was not happy. And if I had the decision, she would have been fired on the spot. An experience that has stayed very fresh in my memory and that helped me not a little when I was doing Quality Management and had the responsibility of getting processes working properly. Laziness in thought and deed was pulled up short.

The problem, of course, was not just the one person actually not doing the work — it was the whole line of other lazy people who passed her along to make my flight a misery.

If you take its immediate impact on relationships, productivity and job and life satisfaction, being engaged lifts life and living from being a drudgery or a millstone, to something fulfilling.

It involves you — mind, body and soul. If you really think about what it is you are doing, why you are doing it and how it fits in the greater scheme of things, it suddenly becomes more meaningful. It is suddenly not a series of unrelated activities and tasks, but a wheel that is facilitating the flow of your life and the world around you. Now isn't that much better than the daily grind?

I have written of intent and how incongruence in intent and intentions is what brings about skewed results. In turn, it is lazy thinking that brings about incongruence.

Really considering what is going on around us, rather than accepting what we are fed, requires effort. It requires us to engage all our senses to gather information, process it and draw our conclusions. It requires our emotional and mental energy.

Lack of engagement causes a number of hiccups in our lives, some so insignificant as to pass by unnoticed and some with grave consequences.

The molding of our relationships is a power we have that is an immense undertaking and one that is largely underestimated or miscalculated. We must spend thoughtful effort in the love, discipline, indulgence, corrections, etc. that is required of us.

How and when do we express each? Which battles should we choose and which to gracefully retreat from? What does love mean to us and how to show it?

These are profound understandings and decisions that impact us and the people around us hugely. We cannot afford to be lazy in this, we must engage.

This applies in equal measure to the relationships beyond our primary ones. We can encompass as wide a world as our energy and inclinations allow and help to stamp out practices that infringe every tenet of good relating.

Like injustice and prejudice.

It beggars the imagination that this should exist in the global village that we are in now. Do we leave it up to judge and jury? Is it "not our problem"? Are we afraid to speak simple truths because it goes against the crowd? Well then, this is what we get. Anger, violence, and hatred that begets hatred.

To be engaged, we need to go the extra mile. To step outside of ourselves and our understanding and embrace more truths, not necessarily greater or lesser than our own.

One of the funnier twists of sayings I've heard is this: If you would understand a man, walk a mile in his shoes. Then it wouldn't matter because you'll be a mile away and have his shoes!

But I digress.

The minutiae with which we surround our lives should not blind us to other parallel realities that exist in the lives of others. In all the travelling that I have done, what strikes me most is how we are more similar than we are different. Shylock's impassioned speech comes to mind — "if you prick us, do we not bleed?"

If we ignore our potential to bring harmony and succour to others, if we merely do our "duty," that is a form of laziness, a lack of engagement that is criminal in its proportions.

At the same time, we must take care to surround ourselves with people who think likewise to maintain the balance of energies.

In all the facets of our personality — physical, mental, emotional, psychological and spiritual — exactly how engaged are we?

# 17

## NOT SO BAD AFTER ALL

**W**e shudder to even think about, and therefore we don't make, the "hard" relationship choices that come before us. We vacillate between the need to spare ourselves and spare others pain or hardship, seemingly oblivious to the current pain and hardship we find ourselves in.

Or it may be that we occupy ourselves finding good reasons for why we cannot act. Let me give you a host of good reasons why you should.

### Because you owe it to yourself to not accept bad behaviour

It is sometimes hard to give up on people even when they behave badly. We hang on to relationships for the false sense of security they might give us.

But bad behaviour at its root could be a symptom of a deep lack of caring. We will never find out which is which until we call time on actions that hurt or offend us.

There is no reason on this earth for accepting abuse on any level and that spans everything from the slighting, spiteful remark, to the roll-the-eye scornful look, to full out physical, psychological or emotional abuse.

All of it takes a toll on the psyche and there is no room or space for this baggage on the way to full evolution. It will trip you up, it will bring you down. Zero tolerance on behaviour that jars your senses.

## Because you owe it to yourself to be in an environment in which you can grow and flourish

If you have gone through *Going Home*, Book 1 of this series and paid attention, you now have a vision of all you could be and all you want to be.

You owe it to yourself to not have that vision sputter and die like a damp squib. The only way that is going to happen is to have happy positive relationships.

No matter what our worldly achievements are in life, it all comes to naught if, when we are in the quiet of our personal lives, we have no one in our corner. No one to celebrate and be happy with us. On the flip side of this, a cheering, positive group of people gives us the strength and endurance to go the distance and make that final step.

The energy of our associations will boost us or flatten us.

It is true that with a great deal of effort and an unusual confluence of circumstances, a person can overcome the worst situations and triumph. And even in that situation, there is always at least one person who had faith and belief in them.

If you must choose, choose growth. Reach for your dreams and watch for who helps you joyously.

**Because you owe it to yourself to be proud of everyone around you**

In the same way, you want to be able to rejoice with your friends, family, business, and romantic partners. You want untrammeled celebrations of their paths and success because their ways of achieving, their ethics, principles, and treatment of others are things you can share in and be proud of.

This is not a question of controversy or the lack thereof, it is about being cognisant of how the people around you live their lives. It can encompass a wide range of being, but if someone does something that makes you cringe, that makes you think "Wow, I cannot understand that in a million years" it's time to wield those pruning shears.

We owe it to ourselves to be able to get behind the decisions our friends and family make and for them to be in accord with all the things we hold dear and sacred.

**Because you owe it to yourself to be loving towards everyone around you**

Let's face it. There are people in this world we just cannot love. It is as simple as that.

The ideas they hold, the lives they live are as repugnant to us as ours must be to them.

Well and good. Leave them alone.

It's a very wide world, and there are plenty and enough people who we can come to care for and love deeply. Fill your life with them, and remove the others.

There truly is someone for everyone, and like liquid, they will all find their own level. So be it.

The capacity to care about each and every one you associate with is a wonderful thing. To know that each time the phone rings or an email comes in, it is from someone you are absolutely delighted to hear from. Yes, it is not only possible, it is imperative to choose to make this true.

## Because you owe it to yourself to create a bubble of joy that is your world

And if you can follow through with choosing at every step of the way according to the above, you will have an unadulterated bubble of happiness that surrounds you. The positive energy that is created from unrelenting peace and joy cannot be described.

The wheels of life move so much more easily knowing that there are no more tensions, upsets, and fights around the corner.

Disagreements, debate, and healthy differences of opinion maybe, that's what keeps life interesting. But under it all runs a deep vein of mutual caring and looking out for each other's best interests. Truly heaven on earth.

In the light of this, any decision that needs to be made to get there won't be so difficult after all, will it?

# 18

## ONLY POSITIVES

The emotional arc of our lives is measured by the soundness of our relationships. If we choose ones that are bound to leave us scarred, we carry with us that baggage and detritus until we choose with some insight and effort to shrug it off.

In the final analysis, we must handle ourselves with care. We are at once stronger and more fragile than we think. We have the strength to make tough decisions and we have the fragility to be badly hurt if we don't.

Do not misplace and misunderstand these two things. You do not need your strength to stay in a bad situation or surrounded by people who crush your spirit. This is an utter waste of your being and potential.

You must draw on your strength to get out. Doing a stock take and following the techniques for change at the end of *Going Home* will help you find your core self and start the rebuilding process. It is there that you must begin.

This is an essential component to building nourishing relationships, that you start with knowing yourself, knowing what type of relating you need in your life and what that would look like for you.

This will help you to critically assess the connections in your life to see if they fit with your true self.

If there are some that are off-key you now have the tools to examine the reasons why and fix any issue at its source. This is important.

It is no longer an option to stick Band-Aids over hurts or whitewash over cracks. You have hopefully reached a place where you do not want to be limping through life with damaged relationships.

Fix them or jettison them.

We want to be left with purely positive relationships. The importance of this cannot be overstated .

Consider the amount of mental space and emotional energy toxic relationships take up. The let downs, the heartbreak, the time consumed to fix things we should never have had to fix.

If all our encounters in our daily life are smooth and uncomplicated, where everyone does what they can, when they can, and all of it flows into a grand design that interlaces perfectly — well, we have a whole lot less to worry about, a great many things we can cease thinking about because the world around us as a result of our associations is proceeding according to plan.

We will have a bountiful quantity of mental and emotional energy to expend on our life's purpose. On growth instead of just survival.

The energy of good relationships expands apace as our associations serve as a mirror of ourselves.

Birds of a feather really do flock together.

So as your friends represent your philosophies and ethos of life, so do theirs and the ripples of trust and enriching friendships increase and flow outwards, till your six degrees of separation hold nothing but people you are supremely content to relate to. Not for the purpose of anything except the joy of community based on shared fundamental values.

When we create societies on this basis of unadulterated goodwill and positivity, we foster and expand a brilliant synergy.

Ideas, creativity, and true solutions are born in just such a mix. When all of these are rooted in reality and spirituality, which is nothing more or less than our true selves, they have the full force of purity of intent, without the pitfalls of ego, greed, or power grabs.

The satisfaction of being able to be and do from this point of source energy is limitless. In this second stage towards our *Core of Steel*, we have now come to terms with our previous conditioning, found ourselves and cleared out and perfected our relationships.

This is a formidable shield to go forward with in life. It gives us the springboard to the rest of our dreams and at the same time a centre of joy and contentment within ourselves.

Which brings me to the final and most powerful reason of all to make every single association a positive one.

Because you are worth it.

Dear Reader

Hello! I do hope you found this book helpful. I implore you to take the ideas you have in your head right now and make something tangible out of them. It typically happens that you can read something and have a glowing vision of your life, but then you get caught up in the hum-drum of existence and the vision fades and dies.

Not this time. This time, write it all down, believe you can make it happen because you can. These books are not intended to give you the equivalent of a sugar high, but real nourishment for your body, mind and soul. There is only benefit to be had by growing into your own truth - for yourself and for everyone around you.

You can take a look at the other books in the series to help you further along the path

Core of Steel The Beginning: Unconform
Core of Steel Book 1: Going Home

I hope you have a wonderful life. I wish you joy and peace.

Penni

## Review request

If this book has inspired you to change your life, please consider leaving a review of how it did so. Your review might help someone else pick up this book and find the answers they need. Everyone's experience and viewpoint is different and valuable and I would love it if you could share yours.

## Connect

Do you have a question or an insight?

You can visit my website or social media pages and post a question, if something has you utterly stumped, or a comment. I believe we are all here for each other and I couldn't be happier if I can help you reach your goals.

Facebook: www.facebook.com/TruthreduxNow
Twitter: www.twitter.com/pmannasd
Website: www.truthredux.com

# ABOUT THE AUTHOR

Penni Mannas Diefendorf is a skeptical dreamer who likes to believe in magic and the impossible but wants proof.

She has done a great many things in this lifetime, but the things she likes best are fixing things, teaching, and learning. Close seconds are singing, dancing, and dreaming, all of which are otherwise known as meditation.

She currently resides in Hong Kong, which is an über splendid place to be, with her husband, who is an über splendid fellow.